NAMES OF
HEROES
OF THE
FAITH

NAMES OF HEROES OF THE FAITH

MARK A. TABB

MOODY PRESS

CHICAGO

ISBN: 0-8024-6180-8

1 3 5 7 9 10 8 6 4 2

Printed in the United States of America

To my grandfather, A. B. Hervey.
He prayed for many years
that one of his five grandsons would be a pastor,
yet he never lived to see God answer his prayer
through the youngest of the five.
I owe so much to my grandfather.
Anything God does through my life
can be traced back to his faithful prayers
and the example he set throughout his life.

CONTENTS

ACKNOWLEDGMENTS

Thank you to my wife, Valerie, and our three daughters, Bethany, Hannah, and Sarah, for their patience with me throughout the writing of this book. Thank you as well to Jim Bell of Moody Press for inviting me to contribute to the *Names of God* series, and to Cheryl Dunlop, my editor at Moody, for her excellent work on our second project together. I also want to thank my church family, the First Baptist Church of Knightstown, Indiana, for giving me the freedom as their pastor to pursue my passion for writing.

INTRODUCTION

Heroes
*Those greatly regarded for their achievements
or qualities; men and women who are admired
for their brave or noble deeds.*

Hero. The very mention of the word conjures up images of larger-than-life personalities, hearty souls who never back down from danger. No mountain is too high, no foe too fierce for them. Ordinary human beings like you and me run away, but heroes stand their ground. They refuse to surrender even in the face of impossible odds. History is filled with true heroes. Lewis and Clark overcame rivers, mountains, record cold, and hunger to cross an unexplored continent. Winston Churchill rallied a nation and a world against the Nazi war machine and emerged victorious. Neil Armstrong did what men had dreamed of since the beginning of time as he stepped onto the surface of the moon. Amelia Earhart, Lucky Lindy, the Babe—all were heroes, fearless individuals who did the impossible.

When we begin to explore the lives of the heroes of the Bible, the picture becomes even more impressive. Throw in the dimension of faith and we find not just heroes but superheroes, world changers, miracle workers. Men like Moses and David did more than heroic deeds; God performed the supernatural through them. Just think of the feats of the heroes of the faith. Some slew giants, whereas others defeated kingdoms with nothing more than a shepherd's staff. Rivers and seas parted, fire fell from the sky, horrible diseases disappeared—all at the hands of men and women filled with the power of God.

I don't know about you, but I'm very intimidated by this crowd. When I look at their lives I feel small and weak. Several years ago I met one of my sports heroes, Tom Landry, the legendary former coach of the Dallas Cowboys. Standing before him I could hardly force words to come out of my mouth, and when I did speak I embarrassed myself with what I said. He took the Cowboys to five Super Bowls, winning two. Standing next to him made me feel small and insignificant. I can only imagine what a fool I would make of myself if I could meet the apostle Paul in person. Or Noah, or Abraham, or Joshua. I'm sure I would plant my foot firmly in my mouth or become so tongue-tied that I could only manage strange, gurgling sounds rather than words. After all, these people are more than celebrities; *they are in the Bible!*

I look at the characters whose lives fill the pages of the Bible and wonder how I can ever relate to them. They seem so strong, so committed; I feel so weak, so easily distracted from the tasks God gives me to do. Daniel risked death in order to pray; I struggle to conquer sleep during my quiet times. And these people really lived. Their stories aren't the work of a novelist trying to amaze us with superhuman tales. Every story in the pages of Scripture is true, from the tale of Cain and Abel to that of Paul's missionary journeys. Fictional characters I can deal with. Their exploits entertain me and may even inspire me, but knowing that Moses actually walked into Pharaoh's palace armed with nothing more than a shepherd's staff and demanded the release of several million Jews utterly astounds me. Who can relate to a man with such courage?

Through the pages of this book, we will explore the eleventh chapter of the book of Hebrews, a very intimidating place for those of us who become tongue-tied in the presence of the fearless. Every paragraph of Hebrews 11 brings us face-to-face with another hero, another person who overcame giant obstacles to do the impossible. It is a who's who of Old Testament saints: world changers, giant killers, saviors. We shrink in their presence, and we wonder what, if anything, these heroes of the faith have in common with frail creatures of dust like you and me.

But when we look closely at their stories we don't find supermen and superwomen leaping tall Pharaohs with a single bound. Instead we find ordinary individuals, people exactly like you and me. They wrestled with doubt and struggled to overcome their own inconsistencies. Their feats may be larger than life, but the characters who fill Hebrews 11 are definitely human. In fact, we can share with them the very thing that made their feats possible: faith. Listen to how the writer of the book of Hebrews begins each of their stories:

> *By faith Abel offered God a better sacrifice . . .*
> *By faith Enoch was taken from this life . . .*
> *By faith Noah . . . in holy fear built an ark . . .*
> *By faith Abraham . . . offered Isaac as a sacrifice . . .*

By faith Isaac blessed Jacob and Esau . . .
By faith Jacob, when he was dying, blessed each of
   Joseph's sons . . .
By faith Joseph . . . gave instructions about his
   bones . . .
By faith Moses' parents hid him . . .
By faith Moses . . . refused to be known as the son of
   Pharaoh's daughter . . .
By faith the people passed through the Red Sea . . .
By faith the walls of Jericho fell . . .
By faith the prostitute Rahab . . . welcomed the
   spies . . .

By faith, by faith, by faith: Each person listed
was commended by God for what he or she did by
faith. The Lord did not stand back in awe of the
mighty deeds they accomplished. He wasn't impressed by their daring and courage. Without faith
they would have shrunk back in fear. Their names
and their exploits would have faded from memory
long ago. But because they were willing to trust
God in spite of the evidence to the contrary, they
were commended by God.

What is this thing called faith that allowed ordinary human beings to do extraordinary feats?
Listen to the definition the writer of Hebrews gives
us as an introduction to the list of giants: "Now
faith is being sure of what we hope for and certain
of what we do not see" (Hebrews 11:1). I find this
to be an incredibly simple definition for such a
powerful force. Faith is being sure of that which we
hope for. Don't make the mistake of assuming that
faith is some sort of force ignited by positive thinking. Being sure of what we hope for does not mean
that if we believe hard enough all of our hopes and

dreams will come true. Instead, faith focuses upon God and the fulfillment of the promises He makes. All of those listed in the eleventh chapter of Hebrews hoped to see the promises of God come true. They hoped for salvation, for deliverance; they hoped to draw closer to God and enter into His rest. Most of them never lived to see the fulfillment of their hopes, yet by faith they pressed on, never giving up.

Faith also assures us of that which we do not see. Very few people have actually beheld God. The Angel of the Lord appeared to Abraham. Moses was given the privilege of seeing a glimpse of the glory of God. These two were the exception. The vast majority of Bible heroes were like you and me: They never saw God, nor did they ever hear His voice audibly. Most of them did not even have access to His Word in a written form. Yet each one was convinced that He exists and that He rewards those who earnestly seek Him.

Being certain of the existence and goodness of God was no easy thing in light of the trials many of them endured. They faced obstacles that screamed out to them that God had forgotten all about them. It is easy to talk about God's goodness when life sails along trouble free, but it is a different matter entirely when you are mistreated because you take a stand for God. In spite of the opposition, in spite of the heartaches and pains, by faith each of these heroes of the faith persevered.

Rather than walk away from their stories as ideals that we can never live up to, we need to stop and listen to their timeless messages. The writer of the book of Hebrews chose a broad assortment of characters in order that we can all find someone we can relate to. I find myself in awe of the writer's genius. Every character, every story sheds a different light on how God relates to creatures of dust like you and me. None of these heroes is perfect. Some of these stories are almost embarrassing. Yet each one takes us back to the same place: faith. Without faith it is impossible to please God.

As we look closely into the lives of the heroes of the faith, we will come away with a new appreciation for the extraordinary possibilities of what God can do with ordinary human beings who are willing to cling to Him by faith. We may even walk away from some of their stories mumbling to ourselves, "If God can use him, then surely He can do something with my life." All that is required of us is faith, the willingness to entrust our lives to God no matter what we may face. By faith we carry on the legacy of the heroes of the faith.

1

ABEL

Breath, vapor, meadow, temporary

> By faith Abel offered God a better sacrifice than Cain did. By faith he was commended as a righteous man, when God spoke well of his offerings. And by faith he still speaks, even though he is dead. *(Hebrews 11:4)*

Early spring in the foothills of central California is a breathtaking experience. From Memorial Day through Thanksgiving, rain never falls. Except in irrigated areas a dusty brown deadness settles onto everything during the annual drought. After what seems like an eternity, the drought breaks, and a year's worth of rain falls during December, January, February, and March. The hills turn green, but the real show doesn't start until early March. Rising temperatures cause California poppies and a host of other wildflowers to come to life. The hills look as if God took out His watercolor set and splashed colors around the way a three year old does on a sheet of paper. I've traveled across the country, and I've never seen anything like it. Sadly, soon after Easter the rains stop, triple-digit temperatures take their place, and the flowers fade to brown overnight.

The climate of Israel is very much like that of central California. The same cycle of drought and rain makes the hills of Judea follow the pattern of the foothills of the Sierra Nevada Mountains. Grass springs up during the wet winter, followed by an array of color, only to be swept away by the hot winds of summer. Watching this cycle year after year prompted the prophet Isaiah to write,

> *All men are like grass,*
> *and all their glory is like the flowers of the field.*
> *The grass withers and the flowers fall,*
> *because the breath of the Lord blows on them.*
> *Surely the people are grass. (Isaiah 40:6–7)*

He used the analogy of the grass and flowers of the meadow to show the shortness of our life spans. All of us walk on this earth a very brief time. Our lives are nothing more than a vapor, like a breath on a frosty November morning. The grass withers, the flower falls, and none of us are permanent inhabitants of planet Earth. The question each one of us faces is how we will use this brief existence God has granted us.

The fourth person in recorded history brings us face-to-face with the shortness of life. Abel, the second male child of Adam and Eve, is a man we know very little about. His entire life fits into less than a chapter in the book of Genesis. Abel set many firsts in human history. He was the first shepherd, he was the first person commended as righteous in the eyes of God, and he offered the first recorded animal sacrifice. But it is for his other first that we best remember him. He was the first human being to die.

His name tells his story. Abel means vapor, breath, meadow, something temporary. Like a meadow that withers under the summer sun, his life was very short. The Bible gives so few details about his life that we will never know what he was like. We don't know if he was a dreamer like Joseph or a leader like Moses or a man of great courage like Elijah. He died so soon that he never married, nor did he experience the joy of fatherhood. After he died his legacy was gone. No one carried on his name; no one carried on the tradition he left behind. We don't even know how old he was when he died. Like a vapor he simply disappeared on the afternoon his brother took his life.

It seems odd then to find his name leading the list of those who are remembered for their faith. He didn't have enough time to become the father of nations or to write volumes of poetry or to save his people. Yet there he is, at the top of the list. The writer of the book of Hebrews tells us that Abel continues to speak even though he is dead. His life was but a vapor, but his testimony has marched through time. He died at the very beginning of recorded history, yet every generation since has looked back at him as an example, a role model. Amazing. His entire life can be summarized in ten verses, yet his life continues to touch the lives of others. What is it that his life tells us?

Abel, the vapor, lives on because of one act: he worshipped God and God was pleased with his worship. He and his brother decided to present offerings to the Lord one day. Cain was a farmer like his father, and Abel was a shepherd. Each presented a gift to the Lord. Cain, the farmer, brought some of the fruits of the soil. Exactly what his offering consisted of the Bible does not tell us. Hearing this story in Sunday school year after year as a child, I always imagined that Cain brought a big bushel basket full of grapes and peaches and all the fruits I like. Abel, the shepherd, brought the fat portions of some of the firstborn of his flock. As they presented their offerings to God, He accepted Abel's offering but rejected Cain's.

What set Abel's gift apart from his brother's wasn't just the content of the offering but the manner in which it was given. Notice what Abel gave: the fat portions of the firstborn of his flocks. We avoid fat today as an evil cellulite builder, but in the ancient Near East the fat portions were the prime cuts of an animal. He also offered the firstborn. By doing so he was in effect testifying that all that he had came from God. He offered the best of the best in gratitude to his God. Cain, on the other hand, simply gave a few scraps from his harvest. The language used to describe his act of worship implies that he was going through the motions. He didn't offer the firstfruits nor the best of all he had, nor did he offer the required blood sacrifice. Cain's offering was rejected because God doesn't respond to people mechanically acting out of duty or guilt. Only those who come to Him by faith find His arms open.

This story is very old, but its message is timeless. I grew up going to church. Even today in the Bible Belt of Oklahoma the streets are deserted on Sunday mornings and the church parking lots are full. Until a few years ago most businesses stayed closed on Sundays. If you didn't go to church, there was nothing else to do. You went, you sang, you listened, and you went home. Going to church was imprinted on me as what a person does on Sundays.

As I look closely at my own life I wonder how

many times my acts of worship have actually been accepted by God. To be quite honest, I often don't even give a thought to how God feels about the songs I sing or the prayers I pray. I try to be sincere, but after singing the same hymns for a lifetime it is easy to concentrate on nothing more than hitting the right notes. My mind wanders to the Cowboys game against the Redskins rather than focusing on the Lord of the universe. Worship becomes automatic, going through the motions because it is expected.

Abel tells us that God isn't impressed by the fact that we took time out from our busy schedule to spend an hour in church. Without faith we cannot approach the Lord. Faith prompts us to give our best, to express true thanksgiving. When we worship the Lord by faith, we don't care about how our financial portfolio will be affected by the money we drop in the plate. Our focus will be on God and God alone, our heart filled with praise and gratitude to Him. True worship isn't a question of emotional involvement, of trying to feel more. Abel wasn't commended for his emotions, but for his faith that resulted in worship that pleased the Lord. His life illustrated the words Jesus spoke to the woman at the well: Only those who worship the Lord in spirit and in truth will be accepted (John 4:24). Abel did that at the very beginning of time.

The second message of the brief life of Abel speaks of the price of pleasing God. It cost Abel his life. I don't want to paint a terrifying picture or imply that entrusting our lives to God will cost us our physical lives. However, focusing our lives on the Lord will at least put us at odds with the world.

Cain wasn't jealous of Abel's flocks; he was mad because his brother pleased God while he did not. God loved both boys, but—and this is a very important but—He would not water down His requirements. After Cain became angry because the Lord rejected his offering and before he took his brother's life, the Lord encouraged him: "If you do what is right, will you not be accepted?" God showed Cain how to please Him. Rather than listen and change his heart, Cain lashed out at his brother. He didn't want to deal with his own sin. Instead he tried to get rid of his brother whose testimony reminded Cain how far he was from God.

A few thousand years later we find Jesus at odds with jealous people God had rejected. When the religious leaders handed Jesus over to the Romans to be killed, they did not act to protect religious orthodoxy or out of genuine concern for the people of Jerusalem. Even Pilate, the self-serving, carnal Roman governor, could see that the Jewish leaders wanted Jesus killed because they were jealous of Him. Huge crowds flocked to catch every word that fell from Jesus' lips. He challenged the Pharisees' place as the preeminent religious authorities. They felt their influence slipping away, and they couldn't take it. Rather than change their hearts and humbly follow Jesus, they chose to try to stamp Him out.

Even in our secular age we still find those who are on the outside of God's favor looking with jealousy on those He has accepted. At the risk of sounding politically incorrect, I will repeat a truth that runs throughout the pages of the Bible: Most of the people in this world are alienated from God. When time ends and eternity rushes in to take its place, most of the inhabitants of planet Earth will be separated from God forever. It's not that God doesn't love everyone, nor does He show preference for one nationality or race over another. He offers salvation through His Son to everyone who will follow Him by faith. Unfortunately, very few people are desperate enough to take Him up on His offer. Most of us are too self-sufficient, so confident of our own goodness that we don't think we need to leave *everything* behind to follow Jesus. We offer Him a little of our lives here and there. We are willing to let Him fill our lives with more joy and peace, but the vast majority of people throughout the world and throughout time aren't willing to go to God on His terms. As a result millions miss Him entirely.

Please don't misunderstand me. I don't want to imply that those who choose to follow Jesus on His terms are in some way superior to those who reject Him. Yet this very complaint is constantly leveled against us. We are charged with being intolerant, uncaring, unchristian—all because we take Jesus' words seriously when He said, "No one comes to the Father except through me" (John 14:6). At the beginning of time we hear Cain saying, "I'll show you who is better," as he strikes and kills his brother. The same hostility continues to keep those who reject the Lord's plan of salvation at odds with those who choose to walk by faith.

Abel's life fit his name. He truly was a vapor, like the grass of the Mediterranean meadow that burns away when the summer heat strikes. Yet in his brief time he left behind a lasting impact. He didn't do a lot. Even his life's work fits his name.

We remember him for one act of worship, only one. He offered a pleasing sacrifice to the Lord, a sacrifice motivated by and given in faith. Beyond that is a mystery. Nothing else is mentioned of his life. His brother receives much more ink on the pages of the Bible, yet even Jesus took note of Abel. Like a breath on a cold winter morning he came and passed quickly, yet his testimony endures.

In many ways you and I are the exact opposite of Abel. Our lives are very long in comparison, and we may even accomplish more than he did; yet our testimonies are like a vapor. What he did mattered and lasted through the ages because he exercised faith. We spend a lifetime trying to build a lasting legacy, yet shortly after we pass away our lives are forgotten. Solomon could have been speaking of our generation when he wrote in the book of Ecclesiastes, "There is no remembrance of men of old, and even those who are yet to come will not be remembered by those who follow" (1:11). Men and women pursue everything the world has to offer in search of meaning and purpose. Most of us place God on the back burner in order to chase our dreams, yet once we catch our dreams we find that our lives have been spent chasing things that don't really matter.

You and I need to listen to Abel, who still speaks long after his death. He calls us to number our days and make each one of them count for eternity. We don't need to build empires for God. He doesn't require that of us. Instead He wants from us what He commended in Abel: He longs for us to pursue Him by faith. It's really quite simple. Our lives are but a vapor. We need to spend them on things that last forever.

Abel still speaks; he still asks you and me one simple question: How are you spending the vapor of time God has given you? If your life ended today, would your testimony live on?

Dear God, teach us to number our days and use them wisely. Grant us the wisdom to spend our brief moment on this earth walking with You by faith. May the testimonies we leave behind live on long after we are gone. Amen.

2
ENOCH
Dedicated

By faith Enoch was taken from this life, so
that he did not experience death; he could not
be found, because God had taken him away.
For before he was taken, he was commended
as one who pleased God. *(Hebrews 11:5)*

The pace is monotonous, the story line depressing.
"Adam lived 930 years, and then he died. . . .
Seth lived 912 years, and then he died. . . . Enosh
lived 905 years, and then he died" (Genesis 5:4, 8,
11). With the exception of Adam, the Bible doesn't
give us any details about the earliest generations of
mankind except the fact that these men lived, pro-
duced children, and died. Everybody died. Like in
a Shakespearean tragedy, the characters walk across
the stage, play a brief part, and die. "Kenan lived
910 years, and then he died. . . . Mahalalel lived
895 years, and then he died. . . . Jared lived 962
years, and then he died" (vv. 14, 17, 20). Their life
spans amaze us. Nine hundred plus years! Imagine
the amount of oat bran you and I would have to
consume just to reach one tenth of the life spans of
Adam's earliest descendants. Yet for all of their
years, the only thing for which many of them are
remembered is that they lived, had children, and
died. If they hadn't lived so long we would hardly
notice their existence. Like we do with the names
in the genealogies in other places in the Bible, we
would skip the list of their names in order to move

on to something more interesting. They lived, they died. We live, we die. Our life spans are shorter, but the same fate awaits us.

Nestled in the midst of the endless cycle of tragedy and death is the story of Enoch. His story starts like everyone else in the fifth chapter of Genesis: "When Enoch had lived 65 years, he became the father of Methuselah" (Genesis 5:21). Yawn, more of the same. We know what comes next. He will live for an incredible amount of time, have other sons and daughters, and die, just like everyone else before him and after him. The circle of life will roll over Enoch just as it does every other human being. Scripture says, "Enoch walked with God 300 years and had other sons and daughters. Altogether, Enoch lived 365 years. Enoch walked with God; then he was no more, because God took him away" (vv. 22–24).

Just as I thought, he lived, he had children, and he . . . *he did what?* He disappeared. God took him. The writer of the book of Hebrews clarifies what happened: "By faith Enoch was taken from this life, so that he did not experience death" (11:5). Enoch beat the rap; he escaped the death sentence that hangs over every one of us. He did not die. As hard as it is to imagine, he passed directly from life on planet Earth to the glory of heaven.

I would like so many more details about this guy. I could sell millions and millions of books if I could discover his secret to outwitting the Grim Reaper. Yet the Bible doesn't give us many details about him. If this were a movie, Clint Eastwood would probably play the part of Enoch. Like one of Eastwood's other characters, Enoch is a mystery man, a man who excites our imaginations more with what is left unsaid than what is said. One day his friends and family woke up, knocked on his door, and found nothing. He was gone. Search parties were formed, and his picture was etched on the ancient equivalent of a milk carton. They probably went so far as to drag the local lake and search the high weeds at the edge of the fields, all to no avail. Rumors started flying, and later they were confirmed: God had taken Enoch directly to heaven.

In some ways Enoch is a curiosity stop on a journey through the Bible. As a part of the hall of fame of faith found in the eleventh chapter of Hebrews, the tour guide at his display always begins with the words, "This is the man who never died." That usually catches the tourists' attention. But there is much more to the life of Enoch than the fact that his life never came to an end. He stands apart from all the other characters who lived prior to Noah's flood because he alone is said to have "walked with God." That may not sound like anything remarkable, yet it means much more than the fact he never died. It sets Enoch apart as a rare commodity not only in the ancient world but in every age.

"Walking with God" is more than a synonym for being religious. It encompasses more than trying to keep some commandments or living a good life. The Bible uses the word *walk* to describe a person's lifestyle. Anyone can talk a good talk, but Enoch walked the walk, for he walked with God. Everything about his life can be summarized with that short phrase. People who knew him remembered him for one thing: He was truly dedicated, just as his name implied. He did more than give God an hour of his time once a week or pray during times of crisis. Enoch lived a life of dedication to God. As the writer of the book of Hebrews noted, he was commended as a man who pleased God.

We carry some stereotypical images of what a dedicated God-follower looks like. Dedicated women have long hair, always wear skirts or dresses, and never wear makeup. Holy men have Marine Corps haircuts and wear horn-rimmed glasses and white socks. They rarely laugh or smile since they take God, sin, and salvation so seriously. Usually we think of them for what they don't do rather than what they do. They don't smoke, drink, use foul language, have overpowering sexual urges, listen to rock and roll, or go to movies. Most of their time is spent at church or in prayer meetings. The most dedicated carry pocket Bibles or lists of the Ten Commandments so that they can be sure never to cross the line into sin.

The problem with our stereotypes is that they miss the point of what is going on in the lives of those who follow the Lord. Enoch stringently avoided sin, yet that was only one small part of the life of this man. The Bible paints a picture of him as a man who knew God in a way that most of us rarely dream of. He walked with the Lord, and they spent time together. Of course Enoch kept the commandments that he knew (keep in mind that Moses' stone tablets were still several thousand years in the future), especially the first and greatest commandment: "Love the Lord your God with all your heart and with all your soul and with all your mind" (Matthew 22:37). God took Enoch directly to heaven because he drew so close to the Father that the Lord decided to remove every barrier between them, including Enoch's mortality.

Enoch departed a long time ago. His lifetime takes us back to an age when the world was young. Times may have changed, but God has not. He still wants to have the same intimate relationship with you and me that He enjoyed with Enoch. Listen to God's ultimate plan for all of us:

> Then I saw a new heaven and a new earth, for the first heaven and the first earth had passed away, and there was no longer any sea. I saw the Holy City, the new Jerusalem, coming down out of heaven from God, prepared as a bride beautifully dressed for her husband. And I heard a loud voice from the throne saying, "Now the dwelling of God is with men, and he will live with them. They will be his people, and God himself will be with them and be their God. He will wipe every tear from their eyes." (Revelation 21:1–4)

Look closely at this passage. It draws a wonderful picture of the closeness God wants to share with us. I especially like the last sentence, "He will wipe every tear from their eyes." It reminds me of some of the tender moments I have with my three daughters, times when one of them comes to me frightened or in pain. As the tears stream down her face, all she wants is to be held. I quickly snatch her up in my arms and hold her tight. Once the tears stop flowing and a smile returns to her face, I love to gently wipe away the tears that remain. This is a perfect picture of the intimate closeness God wants us to enjoy with Him.

Between the time of Enoch and the end of the

world, our Father actively seeks those who will dedicate their lives to Him and walk with Him. We don't have to wait until we get to heaven for Him to live with us. Before Jesus departed He promised to send the Holy Spirit to every one of His children so that we would never experience a moment of being separated from God. Enoch's story reminds us that God loves us and He wants to know us both personally and intimately. Unless we are alive when Jesus returns, we will not escape the physical experience of death, but death is not the end of our lives. Intimacy with God is one relationship that will last forever and ever.

The means by which we can enter into this relationship has not changed since the time of the Fall. Reading the stories of early man as recorded in the book of Genesis, we sometimes get the idea that God was nearer then than He is now. We read of Adam and Eve walking with God in the Garden of Eden and we sometimes assume that their descendants had the same privilege. Cain heard God speak, as did Noah and Abraham. It was easy to believe back then. Angels frequently visited men and women. God's voice boomed down from heaven. Under those conditions who wouldn't believe?

In reality, faith was even more difficult then than it is today. A huge expanse of time is covered in the early chapters of the Bible, during which the population of the earth expanded rapidly. Signs of God's love and care were spread out over generations with wide gaps in between. To complicate matters was the absence of written revelation. Enoch did not have a Bible (not even the Old Testament) to read each morning, nor did he have a hymnbook full of songs of praise and worship. All he knew about God was what had been handed down to him through his forefathers. I find it remarkable that Enoch believed and developed such a close walk with God with so little information. He didn't need much, for he acted on what he had.

You and I know more about God than Enoch's generation ever thought possible. In addition to the Word of God, we have books without number written to help us in our walk with the Lord. We have access to churches and Christian music and retreat centers and devotional materials without end. Yet how many of us consistently walk with the Lord? Our information is so great that we come close to being able to walk by sight rather than by faith. Yet, in spite of all we have, most of us struggle to develop an intimate relationship with our Lord.

We need to go back and take a serious look at the life of Enoch, a man who walked with God and pleased Him. He was dedicated to the Lord. Nothing else took precedence over that relationship. Perhaps this is where most of us fall short. We know a lot about God, and we even claim to know Him personally. Yet most of us have so many commitments, so many obligations of our time and energy, that we have very few moments left for the one commitment that truly matters.

O Lord, strip away everything that stands in the way of my dedication to You. As You did for Enoch when he sought You, tear away the barriers so that I might know You intimately and personally. Amen.

3
NOAH
Rest, salvation, security

> By faith Noah, when warned about things not yet seen, in holy fear built an ark to save his family. By his faith he condemned the world and became heir of the righteousness that comes by faith. *(Hebrews 11:7)*

A few years ago I received a book in the mail that detailed how and why the world would end on October 28, 1992. Somewhere around three o'clock in the afternoon Pacific time, Jesus would return, history would reach its conclusion, and the eternal age would be ushered in: a lot of activity for an otherwise ordinary day. I kept the book since it struck me as a good conversation starter. "Hey, did you know the world will end on October 28?" made a good icebreaker at social functions. The cover of the book was almost as good as what was inside. In order to prove that the contents were truly inspired by God, the front cover featured a photograph of what was reported to be the Shekinah glory of God falling on the prayer meeting in South Korea where October 28, 1992, was chosen as *the* big day. (I'm not sure the photo actually showed the Shekinah glory of God; to me it looked more like a smudge on the negative.)

In case you missed it, the world did not end. The sun rose and set; October 28, 1992, came and went just like every day before and since. Undeterred, other doomsday prophets keep setting dates for the apocalypse. One after another they march on the scene, set a specific date for the end of the world, and sheepishly disappear from view when their predictions fail to come true. If people did not take them seriously they would be a great source for Christian comic material.

I wonder what we would have thought of the first doomsday prophet if we had lived many thousands of years ago during the lifetime of Noah. He also went around pronouncing that the end of the world was near. In fact, he was so convinced of his own predictions that he mortgaged his future in order to build a giant floating barn. Noah must have looked like the biggest loon to come on the scene since some guy started the story of a man who was taken directly to heaven without dying. Who in his right mind would believe that a giant flood would soon come and wipe out everyone on the earth? And who in his right mind would build a 450-foot, three-story boat miles and miles from the nearest body of water? Insanity, that's what it was, pure insanity. Only a fool would believe these wild tales from the crazy old man who spent his spare time herding exotic animals.

This crazy old man, Noah, is one of several fools on the list of those who were commended for their great faith. Those of us who set out to follow an invisible God on a journey to a destination no one has ever seen look sort of crazy in the eyes of the world. We say we have a word from God, a word warning us of impending destruction. Like He did with Noah, God has placed on us the task of saving the world. Only the world does not want to be saved.

Noah's name means rest, but it speaks more of the life he dreamed of than the life he lived. The word *rest* goes beyond ceasing from activity or coming to a stop. The Old Testament uses the term to describe settling down and enjoying security and satisfaction. It is synonymous with another familiar term, *shalom,* peace. Joshua and the Israelites enjoyed such a rest after they conquered the land of Canaan and settled down to enjoy a land that flowed with milk and honey. God promises those of us who walk with Him by faith that we too will someday enter into His rest. On that day we will enjoy the fulfillment of all of the promises He made to us in Christ as God dwells among His people.

Noah knew that rest lay somewhere up ahead, but he could never quite reach it. The story of his life brings us face-to-face with a man burdened with an incredible mission. Environmentalists talk about saving species from extinction, but for Noah it was more than talk. He literally was responsible for the survival of every land-based living creature, including mankind. Long before the invention of the chainsaw he had to cut down enough trees to make a one-and-one-half-million-cubic-foot boat. One and one half million! And that was only the outside hull. Stalls and feeding troughs and storage facilities had to be built inside. As if that were not enough, the entire structure had to be waterproofed in order to withstand a year at sea. Remember, Noah lived before the invention of the tools today's carpenters take for granted. For that matter, he lived before the perfection of most metals. What a monumental task for one man and his three sons to undertake! No, *rest* isn't exactly the term I would choose to describe the life of Noah. Who would even think of stopping with such dire consequences hanging in the balance?

Who could think of doing nothing when the fate of mankind is at stake? God has never appeared to you or me in the same manner that He appeared to Noah, yet He has placed on us a monumental chore with eternal consequences. We too have been handed the task of saving the world. Jesus' parting words to His disciples and all of us ring with the same power that the Lord's words to Noah had. He was told to build a boat, and we are told to "be my witnesses in Jerusalem, and in all Judea and Samaria, and to the ends of the earth" (Acts 1:8). So much time has passed since Peter, James, John, and the others heard these words that we sometimes forget that they still apply to us. Christ left His church on earth to save the world, to take the good news of forgiveness through the Cross to all the world.

Just as Noah's work was not complete until the rains began to fall, our task remains until the clouds part to make way for Jesus' return. Rest? I don't think so. Billions still have never heard the name of Jesus. Many more have heard of Him but have no idea who He is or what He has done. We don't have to go to the ends of the earth to find people who are dying without Jesus. They live next door to us and work side by side with us. Everywhere we look we see them. The difference for them between our silence and our faithfulness is the difference between heaven and hell. With such dire consequences hanging in the balance, who can find time to sit back and pretend the job is done?

There is more to the story of Noah than the ark

and the Flood. The first raindrop did not fall until two months after his six hundredth birthday. The Bible doesn't give us many details about his early years. Apparently he owned a farm and he was busy with the task of raising three sons. Beyond that is anyone's guess. Yet he never knew true rest during this time. He never found the place of peace and security.

We don't know much about the life and times of Noah except that he lived in an age of unmatched depravity. Violence filled the streets, and sexual sin was everywhere. Even those who were supposed to know God did not live like it. After years of intermarrying with those who had forgotten God, even the "sons of God" lived like everyone else. Looking at our generation we often think that the world is too far gone to salvage, but Noah's age truly was. God Himself declared that He was sorry He had created man. As He gazed down from heaven the Lord's heart filled with pain. Nothing could save them; it was too late. The only thing left to do was to destroy them all, wipe the slate clean as though man had never been created.

We already know the story. God saw Noah, the only righteous man on the planet, and saved him. Unfortunately, we forget how difficult life was for Noah and his family leading up to that day. By refusing to live like the rest of the world, he put himself at odds with everyone. Building the ark was a huge task, but it must have been a relief of sorts. He thought he might have a chance to rest while he was on board. Going against the tide is exhausting. Noah had to do it every day. He didn't fit in with the rest of the world. His lifestyle stood out as odd, out-of-date. He must have been the punch line of all of his neighbors' jokes. Every day he cried out to God for action. We get worn down by peer pressure after a few days or weeks. Put yourself in Noah's place. What must it have been like to live as an outcast for six hundred years?

I find our world an exhausting place to live. Temptation is everywhere. Going against the crowd is hard work. I get tired of trying to be different while my flesh wants to give in and enjoy the good life promised on beer commercials. Those of us who try to follow Christ by faith cannot drop our guard even for a moment. We're surrounded by people who would love to see us fall. You've heard them, and so have I:

Come on, what will it hurt?
Why do you have to be so weird about all of this?
It's no big deal.
Everyone else is doing it.
One time won't matter.
How do you know it's bad if you don't at least try it?

When we walk by faith we don't find many places to drop our guard and rest.

Noah found a new adversary after the flood waters subsided. Once the animals were off the boat, he must have thought that at long last he could rest. Finally, the wicked were gone. He didn't have to worry about them laughing at him or trying to trick him into falling. And he didn't have to worry about the animals anymore. It must have taken several years for him to get the barn smell out of his nostrils. Now the birds and the goats and the rabbits and the lizards could take care of themselves.

He was retiring. His work was over. Now he could finally rest.

The book of Genesis records one story of Noah's life after the flood. That story doesn't do much to encourage the faithful. It seems that in his retirement Noah went back to tending a vineyard. The ninth chapter of the book of Genesis records an episode when Noah drank too much wine and passed out naked in his tent. Like I said, this isn't exactly the kind of story you expect to hear about a member of the hall of fame of faith. God in His wisdom includes stories like these to remind us that each of these people is indeed human. Noah passing out drunk in his tent warns us that even if God washed all the evil people out of our world we still could not rest on our journey of faith. Like Noah, you and I will struggle against our own flesh until the day our Lord returns. If the man whom God used to save the world could fall, so can you and I.

Noah, whose name meant rest, found that in this world there is no rest for the righteous. We can never stop; we can never settle down until that day our Lord returns. Only in heaven do we find the place we can finally call home.

Lord, give me the strength to keep up the fight. Help me to faithfully share the good news of Jesus even when the work wears me out. The struggle against sin is almost more than I can bear. Lord, I look to You. You are my rest. Amen.

4

ABRAHAM
Father of a multitude

By faith Abraham, when called to go to a place he would later receive as his inheritance, obeyed and went, even though he did not know where he was going. . . . By faith Abraham, even though he was past age . . . was enabled to become a father because he considered him faithful who had made the promise. . . . By faith Abraham, when God tested him, offered Isaac as a sacrifice. He who had received the promises was about to sacrifice his one and only son. *(Hebrews 11:8, 11, 17)*

Growing up I lived and breathed New York Yankee baseball. I not only knew the entire team roster, but I could quote every starter's current statistics. I dreamed of going to New York to see the Bronx Bombers in action. Yankee pennants and newspaper clippings decorated the walls of my room, and I never left the house without my Yankee ball cap (complete with a cross in the crux of the Y like Billy Martin). During this period in my life I made plans for my future family. The girl of my dreams would have to agree to name our children after Yankee legends. Someday our home would be filled with little Mickey and Reggie and Lou and Yogi. I wanted to bestow a baseball blessing upon my future sons so that they would grow up and star in the major leagues.

God heard my plans . . . and gave my wife and me three daughters. I guess He knew I never completely outgrew my fascination with baseball. (No, I did not choose my girls' names from a Yankee box score, even though one of them throws a natural, left-handed curveball.) My plans may have been a bit out of balance, but the principle behind them was very old. Hebrew parents didn't select names because they sounded pretty, as anyone who has tried to pronounce the name Mephibosheth can tell you. Names were given because they meant something. Within every name was a prayer, a blessing, or a statement about the future of the child. Reading through the Old Testament, I find it fascinating to discover how many times the blessing of a name set the course of a person's life.

Abram, however, did not live up to his name. As if to bless his son with the greatest honor any man could receive, Abram's father, Terah, bestowed on him the title "exalted father." Four thousand years ago children were viewed as a sign of God's blessing, so an *exalted* father was a man doubly blessed. As the psalmist said,

> *Sons are a heritage from the Lord,*
> *children a reward from him.*
> *Like arrows in the hands of a warrior*
> *are sons born in one's youth.*
> *Blessed is the man*
> *whose quiver is full of them. (Psalm 127:3–5)*

But Abram's quiver was empty. His wife remained barren as the years ticked by. The childbearing years came and went; the blessing Abram's father bestowed on him never came to pass.

We don't remember Abram by this name. When he was ninety-nine, God bestowed a new name and a new blessing on him. No longer would this childless man be called "exalted father." God decreed that a more fitting name would be Abraham, "father of a multitude." This is where the story gets a little crazy. Abram filed the documents and had his name legally changed to Abraham. As strange as it sounds, this man of ninety-nine years, a man married to a woman who had just passed her ninetieth birthday, chose to be called "father of a multitude" just because of God's word. There wasn't any logical explanation. Most people were probably surprised. If I had lived next door I would have snickered every time I saw him from that moment on. He didn't choose to go by this name because of logic; he made his decision based on faith. You see, not only did God change Abram's name, but He also promised him, "You will be the father of many nations" (Genesis 17:4). Abraham believed God, and the rest, as they say, is history.

The life of Abraham became the standard proof text of the apostles in their argument against those who tried to say that a man could work his way into heaven. We remember Abraham because of his faith, not his works. At the very beginning of God's personal relationship with mankind, Abraham's experience settled once and for all what it takes to know the Lord. He believed God, and his faith was credited to him as righteousness. The only way you or I will ever be saved is by faith. We too must believe God. Then and only then will we be made righteous.

Yet Abraham's story tells us much more than

the single truth that we are saved through faith alone. The writer of Hebrews selected three critical episodes from Abraham's life to show us what it means to live by faith. Every one of these episodes revolves around God's covenant with Abraham, complete with the promises embodied in his name.

The first episode finds Abraham at the age of seventy-five, shortly after his father's death.

> *By faith Abraham, when called to go to a place he would later receive as his inheritance, obeyed and went, even though he did not know where he was going. (Hebrews 11:8)*

Abraham and his wife were still living in his father's house in the city of Haran when the word of the Lord came: "Leave your country, your people and your father's household and go to the land I will show you. I will make you into a great nation and I will bless you" (Genesis 12:1–2). Hebrews 11:8 makes clear that Abraham set out on this cross-country move without knowing where he was going. Stop right there for a moment. Can you imagine severing all your ties with everything and everyone you know to move more than five hundred miles to an unknown destination? Abraham did not know he had arrived in the Promised Land until God said "stop." He could not call home when he became lonely, nor could he fly back to visit family over the holidays. Once he pulled up stakes and left, that was it. There was no turning back.

Abraham left his home in Haran because he trusted God. Notice I did not say he trusted *in* God, but that he trusted God. I know it is a subtle difference, but it is very important. Living by faith means trusting the Lord totally and completely, even when He doesn't fill us in on the details of His plan for our lives. He continues to call you and me to follow Him on a journey we do not fully understand. Demanding explanations and road maps before we will take the first step indicates a lack of trust, regardless of what we say about believing in Him. Our Lord does not call us only to believe He exists. He demands we drop everything and follow Him. Until we trust Him completely we will never take the first step.

The faith that brings about a changed relationship with God also demands patience, as we see in the second episode recorded in Hebrews 11.

> By faith Abraham, even though he was past age—and Sarah herself was barren—was enabled to become a father because he considered him faithful who had made the promise. And so from this one man, and he as good as dead, came descendants as numerous as the stars in the sky and as countless as the sand on the seashore. (Hebrews 11:11–12)

When God told Abraham to set out toward the unknown, He stated the promise of children to him for the first time. "I will make you into a great nation" embodied the heart of God's covenant with Abraham. It implied that he would someday have many, many descendants. Several years later the Lord repeated this promise with an added touch of emphasis. "Go outside and look at the stars, Abram. Count them, if you can. As numerous as the stars in the sky, so shall your offspring be" (see Genesis 15:5). For the first time the Bible records these words, "Abram believed the Lord, and he

credited it to him as righteousness" (Genesis 15:6).
I find it interesting that he believed a promise that
seemed completely unrelated to sin and salvation
and all the other theological concepts we normally
connect with faith, and that his faith about the
birth of a baby was credited to him as righteousness. Abraham believed that God could give a
child to a man in his eighties, that God could and
would do what He had promised no matter how
impossible it might seem.

God first promised to give Abraham a child
when he was seventy-five. He was in his eighties
when the episode with the stars in the sky occurred. But the promised child did not arrive until
after Abraham's one hundredth birthday. Hebrews
11:11 states that Abraham was enabled to become a
father by faith. He first believed God when He
called out to him in Haran; he continued to believe
through the journey and the trials he encountered
while living in tents in Canaan; and he still believed
when Sarah announced that she was finally pregnant.

Faith is not a one-time encounter with God. It
is a long-term commitment. We believe, and we
must continue to believe. The Lord rarely gets in a
hurry. If our faith is tied to physical results, we will
come away disappointed. When we entrust our
lives to the Lord, we embark on a lifetime of waiting. Most of the rewards that God has for us are
reserved for the distant future when time will be no
more. Like Abraham, we must content ourselves
with seeing them from a distance. Even the short-
term plans God has for our lives rarely come
together quickly. Again and again He tells us to be

patient, to wait. Living by faith means letting God accomplish His plan on His timetable.

The third episode from the life of Abraham is both confusing and disturbing:

> *By faith Abraham, when God tested him, offered Isaac as a sacrifice. He who had received the promises was about to sacrifice his one and only son, even though God had said to him, "It is through Isaac that your offspring will be reckoned." (Hebrews 11:17–18)*

God told Abraham to tie his son atop a pile of wood, kill him with a knife, and burn his body as an offering to the Lord. The Lord of the universe, the Author of life, the One who promised Abraham that one day he would be the father of a multitude, told him to sacrifice his only son. If we stop here the story doesn't make any sense whatsoever. What kind of God would give such an order?

The amazing part of the story is not that God gave the command, but that Abraham obeyed. Early the next morning he saddled his donkeys, chopped enough firewood for the burnt offering, and set out on a three-day journey with his son to the place where the sacrifice was to be offered. For three long, agonizing days Abraham waited for a word from the Lord, but heaven was silent. Once they reached Mount Moriah, Abraham and Isaac climbed the mountain and prepared the altar. "The fire and wood are here," Isaac said, "but where is the lamb for the burnt offering?" (Genesis 22:7).

"God himself will provide the lamb" (v. 8) was Abraham's only response.

He bound his son, laid him on the altar, and

took out his knife to slay him. Only then did the angel of the Lord tell him to stop.

This story doesn't make any sense to us except through the eyes of faith. Sometimes in life we feel as though God is sending us contradictory messages. We don't understand the direction He is taking us or the cost that obedience exacts from us. William Carey, the father of modern missions, lived through this paradox. God planted the burning conviction within Carey to take the gospel to the world, a conviction so deep that he would stand over a globe and weep for the millions of souls separated from Jesus. But less than a year after Carey, his wife, and their four children arrived in India in November 1793, his six-year-old son tragically died.

I wonder how the Careys lived through the grief of knowing that if they had stayed in England, if God had simply left them alone, their son would not have died. I wonder how Abraham mustered up strength to walk up Mount Moriah, knowing that he was under divine orders to take the life of his only son. They survived because their confidence in the Lord was greater than their fears. Abraham was completely confident that even if Isaac was sacrificed God would raise him from the dead. He knew that God would do everything He promised, regardless of his present circumstances, and God had promised that a nation would come from Isaac.

Living by faith means having complete confidence in God's faithfulness. By faith we know that He will do what He says and that He will never contradict Himself. When we do not understand what He is doing or why He is doing it, we must still believe that He remains faithful. The father of multitudes knew that God doesn't always seem to make sense, but he still believed and obeyed. His example calls us to do the same.

O God, I want to trust You. I believe the promises You've made, but I need to learn to trust You even when I don't understand what You are doing. Nothing is impossible for You. Help me to remember that and to wait for You to work in Your timing. Amen.

5
SARAH
Princess

By faith Abraham, even though he was
past age—and Sarah herself was barren—
was enabled to become a father because he
considered him faithful who had made the
promise. (*Hebrews 11:11*)

Impossible. There is no other way to describe it.
Completely, totally impossible. Not only was the
idea beyond belief, it bordered on the absurd. For
years her husband had told her the same thing, and
in the beginning she believed him. But infertility
takes its toll on a woman as the months and years
roll by. Long ago she sat and watched mothers with
their children, dreaming of the day she would join
them. With time she grew to envy, then despise
them. Her arms ached to hold a child, her ears
strained to hear a newborn crying for her. Finally
she accepted the fact that her days were past; becoming a mother was one joy she would never
experience.

Maybe that is why she doubted when her husband came home announcing that in less than
twelve months their years of agony would be over.
Maybe that's why she laughed when she overheard
a visitor telling Abraham the same thing: Sarah
would conceive and Abraham would become a father. Ten years earlier she would have burst into
tears, wondering why her husband would touch an
old wound only to leave her disappointed again.

Twenty years earlier she would have danced across the room celebrating. But now, at the age of ninety, she could only laugh. Impossible, absurd, who could believe such a thing?

Apparently her husband believed it. His name had always reminded them of what they could not have, yet several years ago he made it worse. Since the day of his birth, Abram had carried the label "exalted father." Then one day he announced that God had given him a new name, a name filled with promise, the name Abraham. Abraham . . . Abraham? Why would a childless man approaching the age of one hundred change his name to something that means "father of a multitude"? And there was more. He told her that God had a new name for her as well. No longer would her name be Sarai. From this moment onward her name would be Sarah. Both spellings have essentially the same meaning, "princess," but God had more than a name in mind when He changed one letter in her name. To accept the change was to believe the promise that He gave with it: Sarah would be called princess for she would be the mother of nations; kings of peoples would come from her. Impossible, absurd, a divine practical joke. Yet after her moment of hesitation and doubt she believed. As impossible as it seemed, she believed and the promise came true.

Sarah stands apart from most of the others on our list of Bible heroes. God never appeared to her in a vision, nor did angels deliver promises to her directly from heaven. It would be easy to read the eleventh chapter of Hebrews and skip right over her role in Old Testament history. The writer only makes a passing reference to her, reminding us that she was barren and also past the age when conception is possible. Sarah never played a starring role in the drama of the Bible. That's not to say she was unimportant, but she, like many women in the ancient Near East, stayed in the background.

I think that is why I find myself drawn to Sarah. You and I have much more in common with her than we do with her husband. Abraham saw visions of God and entertained angels. And not just any angels. The Angel of the Lord, literally God manifesting His presence in human form, sat down for a meal with him. Sarah observed all of this from the sidelines. Visions of the Lord and angelic visitors were almost as rare then as they are today. If we wait for them before we will believe, we will *never* believe. Sarah didn't demand equal time from God. She didn't wait until she saw the Lord face-to-face to leave her home in Ur and follow Abraham on a lifelong quest. What sets Sarah apart as unique is the very thing that makes her just like you and me. God's word for her came through someone else. Her knowledge of Him came secondhand. She believed what someone with firsthand experience told her.

All of our knowledge of God is secondhand. I have never seen Jesus face-to-face. My hands have never physically touched the scars in His hands, nor did my eyes watch Him turn water into wine or raise Lazarus from the dead. Jesus made lots of promises to His disciples, promises of forgiveness and peace and heaven. My ears never heard Him say any of them. I was born too late; He was already gone by the time I arrived. As if that were not bad enough, I did not have a Damascus Road type of experience like the apostle Paul. Bright lights never knocked me down, nor have voices ever called out to me from the clouds. The Lord never took me up to heaven to show me things too wonderful for words. Everything I believe about God, everything I know about who He is and what He is like, everything I cling to regarding His Son Jesus—all of it was communicated to me by someone else.

We often find ourselves resenting this fact. We want more. We want to see what Moses saw when the bush burned and was not consumed; we want to hear the voice that called out to Abraham on top of Mount Moriah; we want to experience firsthand all the miracles and wonders we read about in the Bible. But God doesn't operate that way. Reading through the pages of the Bible we sometimes assume that everyone had dazzling experiences where the divine invaded ordinary life with special effects that could make Hollywood envious. Sarah reminds us that this is simply not the case. God never told her to leave her hometown to travel to an unknown destination; He never took her outside and told her that her descendants would someday outnumber the stars; nor did He tell her that her name would change from Sarai to Sarah. She learned all these things from someone else, and she believed. God doesn't give you and me pyrotechnics or visions of glory. In their place we have an ancient Book written by holy men of God moved by the Holy Spirit. That's it; that is all God gives us. By faith we must follow Sarah's example and believe.

I also find myself being drawn to Sarah because she didn't always believe everything God promised the first time she heard it. A perfect case in point is

the promise of her son. Shortly after Abraham in-
formed his wife that God had changed her name,
three visitors came into their camp. One of the
three was the Angel of the Lord. (We sometimes forget that Abraham and Sarah lived in tents throughout
their lives even though God had promised them
something more. They never received everything
God promised them for themselves and their descendants; they had to content themselves with
seeing them from a distance.) As Sarah prepared a
meal for the three men, she overheard her husband's conversation with them. The Lord said to
Abraham, "I will surely return to you about this
time next year, and Sarah your wife will have a son"
(Genesis 18:10). Now remember, the Angel of the
Lord, God appearing in human flesh, said this; and
how did Sarah respond? She laughed. I doubt if she
planned to laugh; it slipped out so quickly that she
was embarrassed that anyone heard her and she de-
nied having done so. The very thought that she
would be able to conceive a child and live through
the pains of childbirth at the age of ninety struck
her as wildly funny.

God's plans are so far beyond our imaginations
that we can't help but laugh. He thinks big. He delights in doing things so far above the realm of
human possibility that until we see them come to
pass we find them absurd. A family in my home
church presents a perfect case in point. They were
poster children for the hopelessly lost. Their names
were synonymous in their neighborhood with alcohol, violence, and profanity. Everyone steered clear
of them, and one neighbor even remarked that the
devil himself lived in their house. If anyone would

have suggested that this family would someday follow Jesus, everyone would have roared with laughter. God and church were the last things this family cared about. Yet during the Christmas season of 1986 the entire family came to Christ. Our church was amazed. They were the last people anyone ever expected to see in church, much less kneeling at the altar giving their lives to Christ. This only made them perfect candidates for the God of the impossible to do a great work in their lives.

Unfortunately, the prospect of the impossible opens the door to a huge mistake, the same mistake Sarah made. God makes wild promises to us, promises so big only He could make them come true, but He rarely gets in a hurry about bringing them to pass. We usually find it easier to believe His promises than to wait for their fulfillment. As time drags by and He continues to tell us to wait, we face the temptation of trying to accomplish God's plans through human means. Simply put, we try to take over for God. We tell Him to scoot over and let us drive for a while. He seems to be having trouble working things out; maybe we will have better luck.

This is exactly what Sarah tried to do ten years after she first heard the Lord's promise of a child. By this time Sarah was already seventy-five years old, but her arms were still empty. Her hopes were raised a decade earlier when God appeared to Abraham and promised to make him into a great nation, but as time went by she sank into depression. Fertility specialists and in vitro fertilization were several millennia in the future. Sarah finally turned to the only option available to childless couples in the ancient Near East—surrogacy. Time made her conclude that God did not want her to have a child. If Abraham was to be the father of a nation, another woman would have to bear his child. As a result she presented her handmaid, Hagar, to her husband and demanded that he try to have a son through her.

Sarah's plan worked, but it was not what she bargained for. The presence of Hagar and Abraham's child filled Sarah's heart with more anger. The impact of her mistake has multiplied with time. Much of the fighting in the Middle East today is between those who trace their lineage back to Hagar and those who come from Sarah. She tried to take over for God, but the end result was disaster.

How many times do you and I try to take over for God? If we are honest we will find that it is far more often than we would like to admit. Rather than trust Him and wait for Him to work in His timing, we rush headlong into schemes that only make matters worse. Many of us find ourselves under a mountain of debt for this very reason. We refuse to wait for God to provide what we need, or we choose not to be content with His provision. There's no difference between you and me trusting in the power of credit rather than the power of God and Sarah's plan to have a child through Hagar. Remember, if Sarah's scheme had worked the way she planned, the promise of her name would have never come true. Hagar, not Sarah, would be the mother of kings and nations. God in His grace did not let that happen. He forgave Sarah's lack of faith and fifteen years later gave her the joy of holding her very own son.

I have been a Christian for many years and I

have served as a pastor for more than a decade, yet I still find some of the wild things God does hard to believe. You can call me unspiritual if you like or you can question the strength of my faith, but I continually wrestle with trying to take over for Him or speed His process along. I find I'm a lot more like Sarah than like her husband. Fortunately for you and me, God shows us the same patience He showed to Sarah long ago. He didn't look for another couple when she laughed at the thought that she could have a child, nor did He reject her when she turned to her own Plan B rather than trust in Him. His patience and grace transformed her laughter of skepticism into joy.

What about you? What impossible things does God want to do in your life? Let Him set your imagination to flight. If He can cause a ninety-year-old woman to give birth, nothing is too difficult for Him to do in your life.

Lord, I've never heard Your voice booming from heaven. I've never seen the scars in Your hands and side, nor have I had visions of angels whispering mysteries too wonderful to understand. I'm like Sarah: Everything I know about You someone else has told me. But I believe, Lord, I believe. Grant me the patience to wait on You without trying to take over for You. Amen.

6
ISAAC
Laughter

By faith Isaac blessed Jacob and Esau in
regard to their future. *(Hebrews 11:20)*

He followed his father up the mountain, but the
weight of the wood on his back made walking
along the rocky path difficult. For three days they
had traveled to this place, and for three days his father had been surprisingly quiet. It seemed that he
didn't even want to make eye contact with his son,
and when their eyes found each other, he quickly
turned away. This wasn't the first trip they had
made together. For as long as he could remember,
he and his father traveled and his father talked to
him about the invisible God and the promises He
had made. He grew up hearing tales about visions
of angels and divine communication. Isaac found
them all fascinating. But his father seemed to run
out of stories during this journey. He wasn't himself. His smile had disappeared, and his mind
seemed a million miles away.

Up they walked, one after the other. Finally
Isaac broke the silence. "Father?"

"Yes, my son?"

"The fire and the wood are here, but where is
the lamb for the burnt offering?"

"God Himself will provide the lamb," his father answered.

Once they reached the top the two of them gathered stones for an altar. Isaac knew the procedure well. They had worshiped together many times, but this time was different. As soon as the altar was finished, Abraham approached his son and silently took the ropes from the bundle of firewood and wrapped them around Isaac. Abraham did not say a word; his eyes said it all: "Trust me. Trust God." Isaac did not know what was going on. Suddenly he realized that he was the lamb; he was about to be sacrificed. Words welled up in his throat, but the look in his father's eyes trapped them in their place. "Trust me, God will provide." And He did.

In many ways Isaac is an enigma to us as we read through the stories of great Bible heroes. The Lord is known as the God of Abraham, Isaac, and Jacob, forever sandwiching Isaac between his father and his son. But we lose him in the shadows of the other two. We come down from the climax of Abraham's life on Mount Moriah expecting even greater tales from the life of his son. Yet as we read through Isaac's life we come away asking, "Is that it?" Some commentators call him a spiritual disappointment. He neither attempts nor accomplishes great things for God. It is almost as though his life story is nothing more than filler between the heroic tales of Abraham and the adventures of Jacob. Of all the characters in the eleventh chapter of Hebrews, Isaac appears to be the least inspiring, the most ordinary, a wallflower of a hero.

Yet this wallflower has an important message

for you and me. His name means laughter, but the significance of his name goes far beyond this single word. God chose this name to remind Abraham and Sarah of their reaction to the news that Isaac would be born. They laughed and everyone around them laughed because the very thought that a child would be born to a couple in their nineties struck them all as absurdly funny. Once Isaac was born his name spoke of the incredible joy his parents felt to hold him in their arms for the first time. News of his birth spread quickly. All those who heard it laughed along, sharing the joy of such an improbable birth. From that moment forward the name Isaac, laughter, served as a constant reminder to everyone he came in contact with that nothing is too difficult for God. The Lord always does what He says; He always provides what He promises.

That last sentence summarizes the life of Isaac. He may not have conquered nations or talked with angels, but he lived his life in total reliance on God. Early in his life Isaac learned that God will provide, that He will do what He promises. Whether standing on top of Mount Moriah with his father or praying for his barren wife to have a child, Isaac walked in simple dependence upon the Lord. He didn't have a catalog full of contingency plans just in case God failed to come through. Reading the story of his life convicts me, for Isaac lived the secret that I struggle to grasp. God is dependable, and He will provide. You and I don't need to worry or panic; instead, we need to learn to trust God.

No story better illustrates Isaac's disappearance in the shadow of his father than the tale of their trip up Mount Moriah. Most commentaries and study

Bibles entitle this episode "Abraham Is Tested," as though Abraham was the only one whose faith was challenged on top of that mountain. Sure, Abraham faced his greatest test—Which was greater, his love for his son or his fear of God?—but put yourself in Isaac's place for a moment. He wasn't an infant or a young boy. The language of Genesis implies that he was a young man, probably at least thirteen or fourteen years of age. As a young man he knew full well what was happening as his father wrapped the cords around him to bind him to the wood on top of the altar. It didn't take long for him to figure out that he was the intended burnt offering.

If my father tied me up and pulled out a knife, I wouldn't sit idly by and wait to see what happened next. I would do everything in my power to save my life. And Isaac could have escaped. Keep in mind that Abraham was extremely old and Isaac was young and strong. If he had made the effort, he could have easily overpowered his father. But he didn't make the effort; he didn't fight back. Isaac knew he was the promised child. His father had already told him how he would someday become a great nation. In spite of his fears, in spite of the apparent contradictions both in the character of God and his father, Isaac took his place on top of the altar, fully trusting God to provide the lamb.

Think back to the last trial your faith endured. How does it compare to Isaac's test on top of Mount Moriah? My trials do not compare either. I find myself panicking or switching to Plan B rather than waiting through darkest moments for God to provide. And He will provide. Isaac and Abraham discovered the power of this truth when the Lord called out from heaven, stopping Abraham before he could harm his son. We may panic, but God never does. He is always in control, always God.

Take a few moments to read through the rest of the life and times of Isaac. You'll find them in chapters 23 through 28 of the book of Genesis. When I read these chapters I am struck by the lasting impression Mount Moriah made on Isaac. Although the events are never mentioned again, the promise God made on that day stayed with Isaac for the rest of his life. Moriah means "the Lord will provide," and Isaac never forgot that fact. The next big challenge in his life was to find a wife. Not just any woman would do. He was the first child of a whole new race, and his wife would need to be someone who loved the Lord. The method he chose to meet this challenge sounds rather strange to our modern ears. He did not set out in search of the perfect woman. Instead he waited for God to provide. One of his father's servants went back to Abraham's hometown, Haran, and found Rebekah. When she was brought to Isaac he immediately married her, and the Bible says he loved her. God provided, and Isaac accepted His provision as the very best.

Twenty years later Isaac and Rebekah found themselves in the same position Abraham and Sarah struggled with: They were unable to have children. How did Isaac handle the situation? Listen to Genesis 25:21, "Isaac prayed to the Lord on behalf of his wife, because she was barren." I love the simplicity of that statement. He prayed. They faced a crisis and he fell on his knees to pray. Do you sense the trust involved? Once again, God provided.

The story line doesn't change with the passing of time. A severe famine struck the land of Canaan, the same sort of famine that motivated both Abraham several years before and Jacob many years after to flee to Egypt where there was food and water. Canaan was the Promised Land even though Isaac did not own a square inch of it. From the day of his birth to the day of his death he lived as a nomad in tents. The logical thing to do, the prudent thing to do, would be to go west toward the Nile and wait for the famine to break. But Isaac didn't do the logical or prudent thing. Instead, he waited for God to provide. The Lord called out to him, instructing him to stay in the Promised Land, which is exactly what he chose to do. Not only did God provide during the famine, but Isaac prospered. The Lord went above and beyond Isaac's wildest dreams.

The book of Hebrews picks up his story at the end of his life. "By faith Isaac blessed Jacob and Esau in regard to their future" (Hebrews 11:20). Listen to the exact words of his blessing to Jacob:

> *May God Almighty bless you and make you fruitful and increase your numbers until you become a community of peoples. May he give you and your descendants the blessing given to Abraham, so that you may take possession of the land where you now live as an alien, the land God gave to Abraham. (Genesis 28:3–4)*

What strikes me is the certainty with which he speaks. Instead of wishful thinking, you hear an absolute confidence that God will give the Promised Land to the descendants of Jacob. Someday this small family will become a great nation through whom the entire world will be blessed. As he looked to the future Isaac didn't wonder whether this blessing would come true. He knew from experience that God would provide. He would do what He had promised.

Life at the dawn of the twenty-first century is radically different from the simple lifestyle of nomadic shepherds several thousand years ago. Isaac never had to worry about mortgages, car payments, or putting a child through college. His generation never gave a thought to corporate downsizing or rising health care costs or any of the other major causes of stress in our lives. Of course, most of us don't have to worry about sneaky, mutton-hungry wolves, drought, or marauding herdsmen. Times change, but God does not. The same God who proved faithful to His promises to Isaac remains faithful today. No matter what we may face, He will always provide what He promises. He will always do what He says.

I believe the reason we do not see greater evidence of this truth is that we avoid situations where we have no other option but to depend upon the Lord. We prefer to see Him provide through the nine-to-five job we go to every day, even if He tells us it's time to move on, rather than to go through the anxiety of not knowing where our next meal is coming from. Walking by faith is not a comfortable experience. It can be very unsettling to know that if God does not come through there is no hope, but this is the way God calls us to live. We need to be more like Isaac. It may be frightening at first, but soon we too will discover that He is faithful, that He always keeps His promises.

Lord, I know You will always do what You promise. You are always faithful to Your Word. I know this to be true in my mind; please help it to become a reality in the way I live my life. Make me more like Isaac. Make me more dependent on You, the One who never fails. Amen.

7

JACOB
He grasps the heel, he cheats, he deceives

By faith Jacob, when he was dying, blessed each of Joseph's sons, and worshiped as he leaned on the top of his staff. *(Hebrews 11:21)*

I admire people with persistence. Nothing inspires me like men and women who refuse to listen to the naysayers and continue pressing on toward their goals. Theodor Geisel was a man with persistence. Twenty-seven publishers turned down his first children's book. They all thought it was a bit odd, not at all like the other books on the market. His style and his approach were unique. No one could see much demand for a story about a cat wearing a hat. No one, that is, until Random House took a chance on a man we know as Dr. Seuss. My daughter told his story to me shortly after the fifteenth publisher turned down my first book. Dr. Seuss's persistence inspired me to keep pressing on.

No one epitomizes persistence like our God. He stubbornly refuses to be deterred from the task of reshaping you and me in the likeness of His Son. It doesn't matter to Him how long it takes or the lengths He must go to. He will do whatever is necessary to make you and me like Jesus. It is a long, painful process, made even harder by our resistance to His efforts. But He never gives up. As Philippians 1:6 promises us, "He who began a good work in you will carry it on to completion until the day of Christ Jesus."

If the Lord ever planned to give up on anyone, Jacob gave Him the perfect opportunity. We find him listed alongside Noah, Abraham, and Joseph as a great man of faith, but faith isn't what most of us think of when we hear his name. He was a schemer, a deceiver, a deal maker. His parents gave him a name that means to grasp the heel, to cheat or deceive, and it fit him perfectly. Jacob was a deal maker, like the slick, stereotypical used-car salesman, someone who wasn't shy about bending the rules to gain an advantage. I find it hard to think of him as a great man of faith. His dedication doesn't compare to Enoch's, he never showed the godly character of Abraham, nor did he ever rely solely on God to provide like his father Isaac. Instead we find him trying to strike bargains with God. Listen to his "confession of faith":

> *If God will be with me and will watch over me on this journey I am taking and will give me food to eat and clothes to wear so that I return safely to my father's house, then the Lord will be my God and this stone that I have set up as a pillar will be God's house, and of all that you give me I will give you a tenth. (Genesis 28:20–22)*

If God will do this and this and this, then and only then will He be my God. Can you imagine someone trying to strike this sort of deal with Jesus when He walked on the earth? I can't. One man came to Jesus and said, "Lord, I'll follow you but first I must bury my father." Do you remember Jesus' response? "Let the dead bury the dead; you must come and follow me" (see Luke 9:59–60).

Wow! Talk about someone who refused to compromise the demands to let someone join the club. But
two thousand years before Christ, Jacob awoke
from a vision of angels ascending and descending a
ladder that stretched to heaven, a vision in which
he heard the voice of God, and he wanted to be a
contestant on "Let's Make a Deal." God had His
work cut out for Him if this heel grabber would
ever amount to anything for His kingdom.

I find that Jacob is closer to the average American Christian than any of us would like to admit.
Many of us come to Christ trying to make deals.
Most of us turn to God so that He will bail us out of
a crisis. On the battlefield such decisions are referred to as foxhole religion; in prisons they are
known as jailhouse conversions; yet all of us fall
into this trap from time to time. We run to Christ
when our marriage is on the rocks or a child rebels
or we face financial meltdown. No doubt we are
sincere in that hour. We mean it when we vow to
come to church every Sunday or devote our lives to
God if He will just fix this mess we are in. Let's
make a deal, God, I'm serious this time. But our
sincerity fades as real life puts our crises in the
rearview mirror, and our priorities shift as daily life
becomes more important than our vows.

When I say *we* I mean *we*. It isn't just the twenty
year old facing serious prison time who suddenly
finds religion. Many of us who claim to be born-
again believers take a very casual approach to our
Christian walk until the moment a crisis strikes.
Then and only then do we get serious about prayer.
We find ourselves clinging to the Word of God like
a lifeline. Promises flow from our lips to God. No

more of this lukewarm religion,; we're ready to get down to business. We're ready to make a deal.

I can't help but wonder how God sees all of this. Reading the story of Jacob, I am amazed that the Lord didn't reject him or turn to Isaac's other son. Jacob was His chosen vessel to carry on the promises first made to Abraham. God did not resort to Jacob's terms, but He did meet his needs. He was with him, He gave Jacob food to eat and clothes to wear, and He took him safely to and from the region of Haran. The Lord went way beyond Jacob's wildest expectations by giving the deal maker four wives, thirteen children, and innumerable flocks and herds (the measure of wealth in the ancient Near East).

Jacob also received something he didn't bargain for. From the day of his first encounter with God he found himself surrounded by his favorite sin. Almost everyone who came in contact with Jacob had an angle, a secret agenda to get something from him. Laban, his uncle and future father-in-law, tricked him into working fourteen years for the privilege of marrying Rachel, Jacob's one true love. In the process Jacob was also tricked into marrying Leah, Rachel's weak-eyed older sister. But Laban was only getting started. He used Jacob to increase his own wealth and squeezed more than twenty years of hard labor out of him.

As if that wasn't enough, Jacob's life was also filled with difficulties and heartaches. With Rachel he endured the pain of infertility and all the desperate attempts to make up for her barrenness. As his flocks increased he endured having his father-in-law turn on him. Later his daughter was raped and two of his sons deceived the guilty party's hometown and killed every man who lived there. Reuben, his oldest son, slept with one of Jacob's secondary wives. On top of this, Jacob lived in constant fear of his brother. Rachel, the one true love of his life, died giving birth to her second child after many years of infertility. Shortly afterward Joseph, his favorite son, was sold into slavery. Jacob was told that his son was dead. He did not know the truth for years. God was with him, yet he endured one devastating trial after another.

Some would call this poetic justice, but something more was going on. God used the trials, the deceptions, the heartache, to chip away at the heart of Jacob. The Lord had great plans for Jacob, and He stubbornly refused to give up on him. All of this finally culminated in a fitful night on the way back to Canaan. Jacob found himself in a precarious situation. He secretly ran away from Laban, taking his wives, children, flocks, and herds with him on a journey back to Canaan. But he knew that if his brother, Esau, saw his face, he would try to kill him. Full of fear and dread, Jacob tried to go to sleep, but a stranger came and wrestled with him through the night. At daybreak Jacob discovered the stranger was in fact the Angel of the Lord. His wrestling match summarized his entire life. From the day of his birth he had resisted God's efforts to remake him, yet the Lord would never give up. On this night Jacob discovered that God would always prevail. It marked a turning point in his life, a turning point that led to the event cited in the eleventh chapter of Hebrews.

I meet a lot of people who are in the middle of

their own wrestling matches with God. All of us
have gone through or are going through the same
sort of fight Jacob fought, although our fight is not
a physical one, as his was. The Lord plans to re-
shape us in the image of His Son. We like the idea
at first. Most of us know that there are a few things
in our lives that need to be tidied up. But the Lord
refuses to confine Himself to cleaning up a few
rooms of our lives; He plans to radically change
every part of us. The biggest obstacle He faces is us.
We fight and resist Him, all the while telling Him
how much we love Him. Here is the good news:
Our resistance is no match for His persistence. He
keeps after us as long as it takes, and He will do
whatever it takes to break and remake us.

This process is neither fun nor painless. Listen
to the way the author of the book of Hebrews put
it: "Endure hardship as discipline; God is treating
you as sons. For what son is not disciplined by his
father? . . . God disciplines us for our good, that we
may share in his holiness" (12:7, 10). Too often we
treat discipline and punishment as synonyms, but
they are not. The root idea of discipline is *disciple*;
discipline is a learning process. God doesn't wait
until we fall into some awful sin to discipline us.
Instead, He actively makes every step of our Christian lives a learning experience.

I find the most painful discipline comes in
those times when God takes my pet sins and turns
them around on me, as He did with Jacob. God
does this with us in two ways. First, He lets us reap
what we sow. By His mercy He refuses to shield us
from the consequences of our sin so that we can
learn to stay away from it. He also turns our sin

around on us by bringing people into our lives who have the same bad habits as we do. That is why those of us who struggle with pride find ourselves surrounded by people who are so arrogant that they're nauseating. Our Lord is simply giving us a close-up look at how we truly are.

God isn't being vindictive or harsh through this process. Quite the contrary. He has a plan and He sticks to it. The life of Jacob shows us that His plan works. At the end of his life Jacob was finally re-united with Joseph, the son he thought was dead. The final seventeen years of his life gave Jacob more joy than all the rest combined. When he was about to die he called Joseph to him so that he could bless two of his grandsons. In his blessing he didn't talk about schemes or slick ways for the boys to get what they wanted out of life. By this point in life he had learned how empty all of those things were. Instead he spoke of the faithfulness of God and the promises He has for those who love Him. Then he leaned on his staff and worshiped the Lord. This was the place God always had in mind for Jacob. His plan was to transform the con man into a man of God, a man of faith. It took a lifetime for the process to be complete, but the Lord considered it time well spent.

God has a similar plan for you and me. He wants us to learn to stop relying on ourselves and our wits and learn to trust Him completely. Through the good times and bad He is not-so-subtly teaching us to lose our will to His. We can resist Him and we can fight Him every step of the way, yet He will never give up. In the end we will find that this is one fight we should have lost much sooner.

The process is painful; I keep fighting what I know I need. I want to be more like Your Son, I really do. Please don't give up on me. Keep breaking me, remaking me in the image of Your Son. Amen.

8

JOSEPH
Add, increase, do again

> By faith Joseph, when his end was near,
> spoke about the exodus of the Israelites from
> Egypt and gave instructions about his bones.
> (Hebrews 11:22)

I have come that they may have life, and have it to the full," Jesus promised (John 10:10). Life to the full—that is what we can expect when we follow Him. Statements like this set my imagination to flight. I want to know more. Full life, abundant life, life the way God meant it to be when He created us—what more could we ask for? Think about the implications. This could really get exciting. Gone are the days of frustration and boredom; Jesus will remove them forever. From this moment forward, life will be an adventure like none we've ever experienced before. Strap on your seat belt because here we go.

But where does the adventure take us? We expect thrills and excitement, happiness and joy, but what does the Captain of this journey deliver? Promises crackle through the intercom of Scripture, telling us that everything we encounter will work together for our good, but does that mean everything will *be* good? We think we know what to expect on the road ahead. Deep down we believe we have some idea of the Lord's game plan for our lives, yet reality is something else entirely. God rarely follows the script we give Him for our lives. He seems to delight in taking unexpected detours. Sometimes we find ourselves wondering if He even knows what He is doing.

Joseph had to wonder this throughout his life. His name means to add, to increase; but for the first forty years of his life the only thing God added to him was heartache. Rachel gave him his name as a prayer asking God for another son. The Lord heard her prayer and granted her request, yet it came at the cost of her own life. Joseph was in his early teens when she died. When he was seventeen God began to work in his life. Dreams came to him in the night promising him a position of great glory and honor. When he told his dreams to his brothers they despised him. They already hated him because their father loved him more than any of them; his dreams made them hate him all the more. Soon they began to plot against him and, when given the opportunity, they seized him, threw him in a pit to die, and then compromised with the one brother who wanted to save Joseph's life by selling him as a slave.

In a few short years Joseph's life went from bad to worse. His original owners sold him to an Egyptian named Potiphar, one of Pharaoh's officials. Unfortunately, Potiphar had a wife who burned with desire for Joseph. When he rejected her advances she concocted a story saying that Joseph had tried to rape her. As if being a slave were not bad enough, the one who dreamed of glory found himself locked in an Egyptian prison with no hope of ever being released.

I find it ironic that throughout this period of

his life Joseph was in the center of God's will. Even when Joseph was a slave the Lord was with him. The book of Genesis says that God gave him success in everything he did, even in his daily service to Potiphar and his household. I know that sounds strange, but let me repeat it: His brothers' attack, his slavery, his time in prison, all happened to Joseph as a direct result of God's will for his life. News like this makes us rethink the whole idea of abundant life. Joseph's life was certainly an adventure. He didn't need to look for the excitement of unexpected twists and turns—he had all he could stand. Yet I doubt if he ever expected his life to turn out this way. His dreams of glory were real. God had great plans for him, because someday this slave-turned-prisoner would save his family from starvation and keep the seed of the Messiah alive. Joseph didn't know that. As he looked at his life all he could see was one trial building upon another, and he prayed for them to end.

Joseph's experience brings us face-to-face with the harsh reality that living in the center of God's will does not always mean a happy, carefree existence. Many of us find that our lives become much more complicated the moment we utter the prayer, "Not my will but Yours be done, O Lord." We already saw how this was true of Jacob. In fact, this same point can be made of everyone whose story is told in the eleventh chapter of the book of Hebrews. Let's review those we've seen so far:

Abel was murdered by his brother.
Enoch walked with God in a time of increasing wickedness.

Noah preached 120 years without a single convert.

Abraham and Sarah anxiously waited twenty-
five years for God to fulfill His promise to
give them a son.

Isaac lived through famines and the heartache
of having sons who hated each other.

Jacob's wife died in childbirth and his daughter
was raped.

When we look ahead we find the same pattern
continuing. Faith does not mean happy endings,
nor does it mean a life free of heartaches, trials, and
pain. If God did not spare Joseph or Job or John the
Baptist from adversity, why would we expect Him
to spare us? Like Joseph we must learn to press on
toward the Lord's ultimate plan for our lives. We
must not give up during the tough times or become
satisfied in the good times. Walking by faith means
pressing on.

The will of God may take us into some very
unexpected, very unpleasant places; yet the Lord
remains in control of the situation. Joseph wondered why his brothers turned on him. He could
not understand why injustice prevailed, forcing
him to spend the prime of his life in an Egyptian
prison. I'm sure he cried out to God asking "Why
me?" and "Why don't You do something, God?" As
we come to the end of the story, we find that the
Lord had a plan in everything that happened to
Joseph. He used them to prepare Joseph for the
hour when he would be exalted over his brothers
and his father. A severe famine was about to strike
the area. The Lord in His mercy warned Pharaoh

ahead of time in a dream. As the events unfolded, Pharaoh turned to a prisoner who was able to give him God's interpretation of his dreams, to Joseph, and entrusted him with the task of saving enough grain during the years of plenty for the kingdom to survive the years of drought. Who better to guide the nation through a time of unprecedented peril than the man who had survived so many unjust attacks?

We often become so panicked in the midst of trials that we fail to see how God is using them. They are the training ground where God prepares you and me for the great works He has in store for us. We shouldn't be surprised at His methods. How many athletes prepare for the Olympics by sitting in a recliner, eating chocolate doughnuts and drinking mass quantities of carbonated beverages? I would love to be an Olympic champion like Michael Johnson or Dan O'Brien, but they didn't just wake up one day and decide to be the world's greatest athletes. Every champion goes through years of grueling, painful, and boring training, preparing himself for one moment of glory. If this is true of those who compete for a prize that will soon be forgotten, how much more should you and I go through the grueling training ground of trials to prepare for a work with eternal rewards?

God also uses trials to prepare us for His service so that, when He does a great work through us, there is no doubt who is responsible. Who in his wildest dreams would have ever thought that the one man qualified to save a nation from starvation was a Hebrew prisoner? Only God. Not only did the Lord use Joseph to deliver the world from famine, but He also used this man to place the sons of Jacob in a place where they could become a distinct nation. If they had stayed in the land of Canaan they would have been absorbed by the surrounding peoples through intermarriage and treaties. But the Egyptians loathed the Hebrews, so they refused to so much as eat with them, much less intermarry. Again, God used the least likely candidate, the one brother despised by all the rest, to preserve their distinctiveness and fulfill the promise made to Abraham. Joseph was the tool, but God received the glory.

When God does a work through us, He does it in such a way as to leave no doubt that He deserves the honor and the glory. No matter how big or how small the task, when God is at work He makes His handiwork crystal clear. Trials, adversity, unexpected twists and turns, all of these give Him the perfect stage to do His greatest works. Too often we forget this truth. We struggle to escape life's difficulties or we wonder why God has abandoned us. Remember the life of Joseph. It may well be that your greatest trial is evidence that God is at work in you.

As we read the end of the story of Joseph, it would seem that his life was a fairy tale after all. Yes, his brothers hated him and sold him into slavery. He was falsely accused and ended up in jail, but in the end he prevailed. Pharaoh raised him up out of the jail and made him second in command of the entire nation. He gave him a wife, a huge house, everything his heart could want. End of story, he lived happily ever after. Yet listen to the assessment of the writer of the book of Hebrews: "By faith

Joseph, when his end was near, spoke about the exodus of the Israelites from Egypt and gave instructions about his bones" (Hebrews 11:22).

Joseph was never satisfied with anything material. You would think that someone with all of his wealth and prestige would be satisfied, but he not only was not, he *could not* be satisfied. His eyes were set on a prize greater than the riches of Egypt. He longed for something more, something only God could deliver. By faith his sights were set on the fulfillment of the promises made to Abraham, Isaac, and Jacob, and he longed to see them come to pass. He knew his body would be buried in Egypt, but he also knew God would fulfill His promise to take His people to their own land—and he wanted his descendants to dig up his bones and take him along.

All of the heroes whose lives we will explore in these pages have one thing in common. They spent their lives chasing a promise that was never fulfilled. None of them received in their lifetimes the one thing they truly longed for. Listen to the way the writer of Hebrews summarizes their lives:

> *All these people were still living by faith when they died. They did not receive the things promised; they only saw them and welcomed them from a distance. And they admitted that they were aliens and strangers on earth. People who say such things show that they are looking for a country of their own. If they had been thinking of the country they had left, they would have had opportunity to return. Instead, they were longing for a better country—a heavenly one. . . . These were all commended for their faith, yet none of them received what had been promised. (Hebrews 11:13–16, 39)*

Joseph's name was essentially a prayer, a prayer that was never completely answered. As a boy he dreamed of what God would do, as a slave and a prisoner he wondered if he would ever see it come to pass, and as second-in-command of the entire Egyptian empire he was still praying, still looking for more.

I find that I am too easily satisfied. I settle for the temporal when God has promised me the eternal. My prayers so often revolve around deliverance from financial jams or help in the midst of a difficult situation that I forget He has a higher calling for me. Joseph's life revolved around God's promises. He would not settle for anything less than seeing them come to pass. Why should you and I be any different?

O Lord, You know how much I hate the pain of training. The days feel like they will never end, and the pain almost becomes more than I can bear. Keep my sights set on the race You have laid before me. I know that without the painful training ground of trials I will never reach the goal You prepared me for. Give me patience, give me endurance, and keep my eyes set on You. Amen.

9

AMRAM AND JOCHEBED, THE PARENTS OF MOSES
Exalted people and *Yahweh's glory*

> By faith Moses' parents hid him for three
> months after he was born, because they saw
> he was no ordinary child, and they were not
> afraid of the king's edict. (*Hebrews 11:23*)

If you are a Christian I'd like to ask you a very personal question: Why do you follow Christ? More simply, why do you believe in God? Why do you go to church, pray, and read your Bible? Why do you believe? Think about that for a moment. While you are thinking, let me ask you a more difficult question: Would you still believe if you had nothing to gain from it? I can hear the chorus of "Well, of course" coming from the nearest Sunday school classroom, but if we faced a situation where this question was more than theory, what would our response be?

A young family found itself face-to-face with this question a long time ago. Everything about their lives told them that God had forgotten them. From the time the parents were young children, they had heard stories about how God chose their people from among all the nations on Earth. He promised to give them a special land someday, a land that was said to flow with milk and honey. In that land all of their dreams would come true. But the stories just seemed like fairy tales now. Centuries had gone by since anyone had heard from

God, and in the intervening time His "chosen people" had been reduced to a nation of slaves. Their slave masters oppressed them, and the king terrorized them by killing their children indiscriminately. For years the people prayed for relief, and for years it seemed as if their prayers fell back to the ground unanswered.

Given this situation, would you believe in a good and loving God? Could you possibly think that He cared for you? Millions of people around the world today find themselves in very similar circumstances. From the inner cities of America to the Third World, life is hard with no relief in sight. We can tell those who suffer that their lives will take a distinctive turn for the better if they will only believe in the Lord Jesus Christ, but you and I both know that there is no guarantee of that. Let's mentally trade places with them for a moment. How firm would our faith be if our misery never ended?

Until we begin to look at the question of faith in a good and benevolent God through the eyes of those who live in unending despair, we can never fully appreciate the faith of Moses' parents. They were born in Egypt nearly three hundred years after Jacob moved his family there under the direction of Joseph. After the death of Joseph, a new king rose to power who saw the growing Hebrew population as a threat to national security. In response he enslaved Jacob's descendants and began the oppression that grew more severe with each successive Pharaoh. By the time Moses was born things had become so bad that the Egyptians were tossing all Hebrew male babies into the Nile River.

The prevailing attitudes among the Hebrews

were fear, anger, and despair. They had gone beyond thinking God had abandoned them. For the most part, they had abandoned God. More accurately, they had forgotten all about Him. Read through the book of Exodus and observe how ignorant Israel was of God. During their captivity in Egypt they had adopted many of the religious practices of their oppressors. Things had become so bad that Moses had to ask God at the burning bush, "Suppose I go to the Israelites and say to them, 'The God of your fathers has sent me to you,' and they ask me, 'What is his name?' Then what shall I tell them?" (Exodus 3:13). It wasn't Pharaoh who would wonder who this God was—it was the Israelites themselves.

Let's pose the question that started this chapter to the Levite couple Moses was born to. In light of their circumstances, why would they believe? Their names give us our first clue. Moses' father bore the name Amram, a name that means "exalted people." His mother's name was Jochebed, which means "the Lord's glory" or "Yahweh's glory." (Their names are given in Exodus 6:20.) These strike me as very strange names for oppressed slaves. A nation of slaves is not exactly the sort of people you consider to be exalted. Nor would it seem that the Lord could derive much glory from people who grovel in mud pits making bricks. Their names sound like wishful thinking . . . or statements of faith. The name Jochebed is a bold declaration of faith in Yahweh, the invisible God, the one true Lord over all. Amram speaks of the promises of God. Only someone who firmly believed the covenant first made with Abraham could say that these slaves would one day be exalted.

The names of Moses' parents reveal one of the most common reasons we believe in Jesus: We copy the faith of our parents. I first heard the story of God creating everything out of nothing from my mother. My parents took me to church on a regular basis and read the Bible to me before I went to sleep. Not only did my parents believe, but my grandparents were also strong Christians. Believing in Jesus was the natural thing for me to do as a child; it was a family tradition. Studies show that the vast majority of Christians were saved before their eighteenth birthday.

But carrying on a family tradition doesn't last long under the stress of reality. Something more than a hand-me-down faith caused Amram and Jochebed to defy Pharaoh and preserve the life of their child. The book of Exodus emphasizes the uniqueness of their actions. We could explain away their hiding Moses to keep him from being killed as the desperate measures of parents who loved their child, yet that explanation forgets the rest of the story. At the age of three months Moses was put into a basket boat and placed among the reeds in the Nile. His older sister Miriam watched from a distance to see what would happen to him. Love can't explain this. Why would they place him in the river? Why wouldn't they continue hiding him or try to escape Egypt to save his life? By placing Moses in a basket boat, they were in effect putting him in God's hands. They knew this was no ordinary child. Because they sensed God had plans for Moses, they entrusted their infant to God.

These were bold steps for a couple who saw very little tangible proof of God's faithfulness. I know we can talk about the spiritual benefits of following the Lord. We can talk about heaven and inner peace and fellowship with God and all of that, but let's face it, their lives were horrible. No one in his right mind would want to trade places with them. For Amram and Jochebed, believing in God was not convenient, profitable, popular, or, in light of their circumstances, logical. We cannot look at their lives and point to something as the reason they believed. Some would say that believing gave them something to pull them through the hard times they faced. If that were the case, why would they believe in the Lord of slaves? Believing in the gods of the Egyptians made much more sense. If they were just "believing" for emotional comfort, wouldn't they believe in something that appeared to work? Their faith did not deliver them from the brick pits or the lash; it did not exempt them from Pharaoh's orders. God wasn't a means to an end. For them to believe required the firm conviction that regardless of what their world communicated to them, the Lord alone is God.

Amram and Jochebed defy most of our modern definitions of faith. Many of us would fail the test Satan posed to God regarding Job when he asked, "Does Job fear God for nothing?" (Job 1:9). The devil contended that the day Job lost his houses and flocks and children would be the day he turned away from God. I'm afraid he would probably be right if that question were raised about one of us. Many of us do fear God for the material blessings we can get from Him. If we lost our health or our jobs or our children and everything else we cling to in this life, we would curse God to His face.

Yet as followers of Jesus Christ we should have already lost everything. In the third chapter of the book of Philippians we read these words, "I consider everything a loss compared to the surpassing greatness of knowing Christ Jesus my Lord" (v. 8). When we know Christ we are to regard everything else as rubbish. We are to freely lose everything to Him. For the vast majority of us this remains a spiritual theory, an ideal we never have to put to the test. But it must become more than that. Is faith that evaporates in the face of adversity really faith at all?

At the beginning of this chapter I posed this question to you: Would you continue to believe if God did not make a tangible difference in your life? What would become of your faith if day-to-day reality continued to spiral downward? What if your most desperate prayers seemed to go unanswered? What if you had to watch your children suffer as well? What would you do then? Would you still cling to the Lord? Amram and Jochebed did. Will you?

Would I still believe? You know, Lord, how I want to think I would. But the prospect of going through the sort of trials Amram and Jochebed faced fills me with dread. Strengthen my faith, Lord. I know that unless Your hand holds me up I will surely fall. Amen.

10

MOSES
Drawn out of the water

By faith Moses, when he had grown up, refused to be known as the son of Pharaoh's daughter. He chose to be mistreated along with the people of God rather than to enjoy the pleasures of sin for a short time. He regarded disgrace for the sake of Christ as of greater value than the treasures of Egypt, because he was looking ahead to his reward. By faith he left Egypt, not fearing the king's anger; he persevered because he saw him who is invisible. By faith he kept the Passover and the sprinkling of blood, so that the destroyer of the firstborn would not touch the firstborn of Israel. *(Hebrews 11:24–28)*

From Genesis to Revelation, people are constantly leaving cozy, comfortable places to follow God's will. Abraham left Ur of the Chaldees to go to a land he had never seen. Jacob left Canaan to find relief from famine. Four hundred years later Jacob's descendants (then two million strong) left Egypt to go back to Canaan. Samuel left his mother to serve in the temple. David left his family to serve Saul. Jesus left heaven to come to earth. James and John, Andrew and Simon left their respective family fishing enterprises to follow Jesus. Matthew left his tax collection booth to become a disciple. Jesus left the disciples to go back to heaven, but He promises to return. Saul, who became Paul, left a promising career as a rabbi to become the Apostle to the Gentiles.

When Christ comes back His church will leave to meet Him in the air.

When I first set out to write this chapter, I planned on putting us on this list. I wanted to explore all the things we have to leave behind to follow Jesus. But as I began to explore my own life, I found that my experience pales in comparison to that of Moses or Paul. Let's look closely at the life of Moses and you will see what I mean.

The writer of Hebrews refers to Moses eleven times throughout the book. Moses' section in the eleventh chapter is second in length only to Abraham's. One idea leaps off the page as a person reads the paragraph devoted to the great lawgiver: He left.

> . . . he left the household of his adopted mother, the daughter of Pharaoh.
> . . . he left the treasures of Egypt.
> . . . he left the land of Egypt.
> . . . he left his father-in-law in the wilderness to deliver the Hebrews from slavery.

Faith sent Moses packing. What sets him apart is what he left behind.

People still leave things behind to follow Christ today. Most of us leave negative habits or destructive lifestyles, things we needed to abandon even if we did not set out after Jesus. Some of you have left family and friends and everything you held dear because you chose to love Christ. But most of us give up very little for Him. I gave up bitterness and anger when I got serious about God—hardly a huge sacrifice. A close friend of mine gave up alcoholism; another friend walked away from a life of

crime. A common thread runs through most of our
stories: We gave up something bad and destructive
in exchange for a better life. Not Moses.

Moses left behind a huge list of positives in exchange for negative treatment for God's sake. When
he refused to be known as the son of Pharaoh's
daughter, he walked out on the woman he had regarded as his mother for forty years. He also left
behind prestige and honor. His Egyptian name,
Moses, placed him in the bloodline of the Pharaohs.
Someday he may have ruled Egypt or, at the very
least, he would have enjoyed a position of promi-
nence and comfort. When he turned his back on
the royal family, he left behind riches. Even the
"pleasures of sin" have more to do with the lavish
lifestyle of the Egyptians than with something obviously bad, like drug addiction.

Moses' life did not improve after he chose to be
counted with the Hebrew slaves. Never again did
he have a solid roof over his head. For forty years in
Midian and for forty more years leading the children of Israel across the Sinai peninsula, he lived in
tents. In exchange for riches, he received disgrace;
for the pleasures of Egypt, he received mistreat-
ment, both from the Egyptians and from his own
countrymen.

Moses could not forget what it cost him to
serve the Lord. His name continually reminded him
of all that he left behind. Abraham got a new name
after he started serving God, a name that looked
forward to all God had in store for him. So did Peter and Matthew and Paul. Not Moses. Pharaoh's
daughter gave him his name when she found him
in the Nile. "Moses" was a common element of the

names of the Pharaohs and their descendants. The
Lord never changed it. He didn't give him a more
appropriate Hebrew name. Abraham's name assured him of God's promises, Peter's and Paul's
names reflected God's calling, but Moses' name reminded him of all he left behind to live in tents
with two million people who blamed him for their
misery.

Our perspective on God would abruptly change
if we were suddenly transported to other spots on
the globe. Iranian believers choose Christ at the risk
of their own lives. Because of the Islamic Revolution
it is illegal to convert from Islam to Christianity. The
penalty is death. Christians in Communist China
face daily persecution. If they openly profess their
faith they will at best be relegated to second-class
jobs and opportunities. Many believers are sent
away to reeducation camps until they see the light
of Marxism. From Vietnam to Peru to the Middle
East and around the world, according to some his-
torians more people have died for the cause of
Christ during the twentieth century than in the pre-
vious nineteen centuries combined.

I used to think it was a blessing to live in a land
where we don't have to give up much to follow
Christ. Now I'm not so sure. Don't get me wrong—I
don't want this year's church youth camp to be in
the local prison. But I also know that the more
something costs me, the more I treasure it. I have
an old car that costs me very little, which shows in
the way I treat it. It's lucky if I wash it once a year,
and I doubt if I will ever wax it. Every six months
or so I drag the trash out of the backseat. An oil
leak keeps me from ever getting lost. The driver's

seat is held in place by a twisted coat hanger. When someone backed into the plastic front bumper, I simply cut off the broken pieces. I never lock it or worry about it. The thing is almost worthless according to the newest blue book. And I value it according to its worth. When following Christ comes cheap, our commitment to Him reflects it.

Moses gave up a lot to follow God, but we never hear any regret on his part. The people he led constantly clamored to go back to Egypt, yet you never hear those words fall from Moses' lips. The rest of the people left the hard life of slaves; he left the riches of a prince. They continually thought about the leeks and onions they had enjoyed during their breaks from making bricks without straw; Moses never gave a thought to the pleasures he formerly enjoyed. He didn't have time to look back because he was too busy looking ahead. Everything he had in Egypt was only temporary, and his heart longed for something permanent. No one's losses could compare to the price Moses paid to pursue God. Yet he had the fewest regrets.

The writer of Hebrews includes one act of faith that confirms Moses' forward vision. By faith he kept the Passover. At first glance it is hard to see how this fits with the other recorded acts that concentrate on leaving something behind. That is, it is hard until we factor in the significance of the Passover. Not only did it commemorate God's greatest act of salvation in the Old Testament, but it also looked forward to a time when His salvation would be completed. From a New Testament perspective we know that it foreshadowed Christ, the ultimate Passover lamb. I doubt if Moses understood all of these implications, but he did know that this celebration would link all future generations of believers back to the first generation who sprinkled the blood on their doorposts. The Passover, God's salvation, pushed what lay behind out of his mind. He knew the time of living in tents would pass and all of God's promises would one day come true. Nothing in Egypt could ever compare to what lay ahead.

I know it feels like we give up a lot to follow Christ, and some of us do. Those who were raised in Islam, or Mormonism, or one of the other non-Christian religions know what it means to leave everything behind to follow Christ. Even those raised in the church who have never known anything but Christian lifestyles see others indulging their sinful desires and saying that Christians are missing out, and sometimes it's tempting to believe they're right. Sometimes believers have to give up good jobs based on their refusal to compromise moral convictions. And following Christ takes a commitment of time and money we'd often rather spend on our own pleasures. Yet nothing we give up can compare to what lies ahead.

Following Christ does make us strangers and aliens in our world. Sometimes this leaves us very lonely, very out of place. Here is the good news. We *are* aliens in this world because our real home lies in the world to come. Remember the words of the apostle Paul, "But one thing I do: Forgetting what is behind and straining toward what is ahead, I press on toward the goal to win the prize for which God has called me heavenward in Christ Jesus" (Philippians 3:13–14). Moses reminds us of the cost of following Christ, but he also reassures us that it is a bargain in light of what we gain.

Dear Lord, my sacrifices sometimes seem so great until I look at them from Your perspective. Nothing can compare to knowing You; no price is too great to pay. Loosen my grip on my world that I might pursue You. Amen.

11

THE PEOPLE OF ISRAEL
He strives with God

> By faith the people passed through the
> Red Sea as on dry land; but when the Egyp-
> tians tried to do so, they were drowned. By
> faith the walls of Jericho fell, after the people
> had marched around them for seven days.
> (Hebrews 11:29–30)

I find it difficult to remain objective when reading
the Old Testament. Many of the stories about the
nation of Israel make me want to yell, "Don't you
people get it?" This may sound a bit disrespectful,
but the Israelites acted like fools most of the time.
Were they brain-dead or what? Wouldn't you think
they would finally figure out once and for all that
the Lord is God? But no, they kept wavering back
and forth between God and popular culture. One
day they were praying to the Lord and making all
sorts of vows to serve Him forever. Then we turn
the page and find them right back on their faces,
worshipping Baal or Molech or a golden cow. No
wonder God became so frustrated with them. Who
wouldn't?

Of course, we never act like Israel did in the
Old Testament by wavering in our commitment to
the Lord. Well . . . uh . . . hardly ever. But that's different. Israel had prophets like Moses, giving
instructions directly from God. All we have is the
Bible, a book of instructions from . . . uh, well our
situation is still different. Israel saw miracles all the

time. Well, maybe not all the time. Actually, I guess
miracles were pretty rare back then too. But we
never see any, well, hardly ever. All right, we see
God at work all the time in the world, but, well, uh
. . . that's different. OK, now I have it. They kept
running back to idols, trying to be like everyone
around them. We don't worship idols; we never let
something come between us and the Lord. We
don't try to be like everyone else. No, not at all . . .
except maybe in the clothes we wear, but that's all
. . . or maybe in the music we listen to and the
shows we watch on television, but we don't worship the world's idols . . . at least not very often.

This is why I find it so difficult to remain objective when I read the Old Testament stories. Israel
frustrates me because my own inconsistencies frus-
trate me. I want to scream at the Hebrews, asking
them when they will finally get a clue; but they
scream back, asking me the same question. Israel
during its pilgrimage through the wilderness is a lot
like you and me. Israel's name comes from the new
name God gave to Jacob, the father of the Israelites,
and it literally means "one who wrestles with God."
Often we find ourselves wrestling with Him, fighting the work He wants to accomplish in us. God
had a plan for Israel. His goal was to take His people from spiritual infants who only turned to Him
when they had no other choice, and transform
them into a nation of people who walked by faith.
It should come as no surprise to find that God has
the same plan for each of us. The process sometimes
feels like we're wandering around, not knowing
where we are or where we are going, sort of like the
Israelites in the wilderness. We can learn a lot from

their experience as they followed the Lord out of Egypt en route to the Promised Land.

The writer of the book of Hebrews refers to two key events when the people of Israel acted in faith. Both are favorite stories of every child in Sunday school. The first came shortly after they marched triumphantly out of Egypt under the leadership of Moses. Ten plagues had struck Pharaoh and his people, leaving them broken and defeated and allowing the people of Israel to leave victorious. But Israel's victory party didn't last long. Pharaoh rallied his troops and pursued the children of Israel to the Red Sea. The people were trapped. On one side was death by the sword; on the other, death by drowning. They panicked, but God did not. He told Moses to stretch out his hands over the sea and, as he did, the sea parted. A wind blew from the east and the waters stood up like a wall on either side, leaving a trail of dry ground as an escape route for the Hebrews.

The second event occurred forty years later, but it was just as spectacular. After the Israelites finally entered the Promised Land they came face-to-face with their first major obstacle, the city of Jericho. The city was encircled by thick walls. Most sieges against walled cities used ramps and battering rams, but Joshua, the commander of Israel's armies at that time, didn't have any of these. As armies go, he was ill equipped to undertake a task as formidable as attacking a walled city. This minor detail did not stop God from ordering the attack. The Lord instructed Joshua to have the people march around the city in complete silence once a day for six days. The only sound was to be the priests blowing trumpets. On the seventh day they were to march around the city seven times, then the people were to shout, the trumpets were to blow, and the walls would come tumbling down. Joshua and the people obeyed, and the city of Jericho fell.

These two events are separated by more than time. The difference in the spiritual maturity of the people is remarkable. At the Red Sea the people of Israel were little more than spiritual infants. When they saw Pharaoh's armies on the horizon they panicked. "Was it because there were no graves in Egypt that you brought us to the desert to die?" they yelled to Moses. This is hardly a firm statement of faith. Yet God rescued them. The sea did not part because of their faith; God acted in spite of them. However, walking through the sea required a great deal of faith, as well as a good measure of fear of the Egyptian army. It was a learning experience and a turning point. From that moment forward Pharaoh never troubled them again, and they knew that God would not abandon them. Unfortunately, in little more than a few days we find them complaining again. Somehow they forgot the lesson they learned at the sea. They ran out of water, so everyone was about to die of thirst (they thought). Once again God came through and gave them what they needed.

We start out on our spiritual pilgrimage as infants. By faith we trust Christ to forgive our sins and adopt us into His family, but we still have a lot to learn about what it means to live by faith. It is easy for us at that stage to believe God for the big things in life. His goal is to teach us to lean on Him for everything. Can you relate to Israel standing on the shore of the sea? I can. Trouble strikes and we panic. It may be the loss of a job, or unexpected medical expenses, or something even bigger; but whatever it is, it threatens to upset the entire flow of our lives. Our first response is to wonder why God would let this happen. We look everywhere we can for a way out, only to find every avenue blocked. Finally we turn to God, and, surprise! He comes through.

Through these experiences the Lord is gently teaching us that He is faithful. Moreover, He is working to remove all of the props we rely on so that we will learn to lean on Him alone. He isn't being harsh or spiteful—far from it. God knows what we need, and more than anything we need Him. He saved us that we might know Him and bring Him glory. Therefore, He rearranges the events in our lives to make that possible. Look back at the Red Sea. Who received the glory? God. Think back to crisis situations that have struck your life. They are opportunities for God to repeat what He did in the middle of the Sinai desert.

God would not leave Israel as infants, nor will He leave us at that level. From the Red Sea to Mount Sinai, where the law was given, the people of Israel faced a series of crises, each of which was designed to teach them to walk by faith. They ran out of food, they ran out of water, and they were attacked by the Amalekites. Every time trouble came, the people panicked, but God delivered them. After they arrived at Sinai He began to teach them through His word. The Ten Commandments and the rest of the law were given to Moses on top of the mountain. Moses, in turn, taught God's law to the people.

The heart of the law's requirements was faith. Out of His mercy and grace God chose Israel to be His people. By faith He was to be their God. The law showed them how they were to walk with Him. This marked a genuine turning point in their relationship with Him. After their two years at Mount Sinai, God no longer dealt with them as infants. Correction was mixed in with the miracles that delivered them from their complaints, because He had big plans for His people. He knew what waited for them on the other side of the Jordan River—He knew the battles they would face, but also the great victories He would give them. They would never see any of it until they learned to walk by faith as mature believers.

We remember how Israel spent forty years wandering around in the desert, but we forget that God's original plan was for the trip to only last two years. They failed to learn the lessons. What choice did God have but to repeat them over and over and over again? When He first brought them to the Promised Land, they took one look at the Canaanites and decided to run back to Egypt. They knew they could never defeat armies that made them look like grasshoppers. And that was the point. They could not, but God could. He proved that forty years later in Jericho when they finally had learned—at least temporarily—to trust Him.

During our pilgrimage with God He has a lot of lessons He wants to teach us. He wants us to learn from Israel's example and stay away from sexual immorality and idolatry (see 1 Corinthians 10:7–8), but He wants us to go beyond simply avoiding sin. Our Lord wants us to walk with Him by faith. Impossible situations lie ahead of us, and He wants to use us to tear them down. Nations on the other side of the globe are closed to the gospel, and He wants to use us to share the light of Christ with them. Huge barriers of racism and hatred divide our nation; He wants to break them down through us. Our God is the God of the impossible. He delights in doing what the critics say cannot be done, but He never does these things alone. He invites us to join Him and be a part of His eternal plan. Like He did for Israel, God has made big plans for you and me, plans we have to grow up to experience.

If the group of people who passed through the Red Sea had arrived at Jericho, they never would have taken the first step around its walls. I can just hear what they would say: "What if they throw rocks on our heads while we are walking by? What will we do then? What if the walls hit us when they fall? What do you have planned, Moses, to keep that from happening? What if they come out of the city and chase us? Who will protect us?" That group of people never came close to Jericho. They all died in the wilderness because they refused to learn from God. They refused to grow up.

It may well be that the reason we don't see God do more in our nation is that He is still waiting for a people who are willing to trust Him to do the impossible. Spiritual infants don't win spiritual battles. Only the mature will stand their ground and trust God to come through. We long to see the spectacular, but God wants us to trust in Him when we see nothing happening. He will continue repeating the lessons until we finally learn them. Israel took forty years to learn what it should have learned in two. Let's not make the same mistake.

O God, when I wrestle against You, I am fighting a battle I desperately need to lose. Soften my heart that I might learn the lessons You teach. I'm tired of crawling like an infant. By Your grace and power, I pray that soon I will learn to walk by faith. Amen.

12
RAHAB
Wide, large open space

> By faith the prostitute Rahab, because she
> welcomed the spies, was not killed with those
> who were disobedient. *(Hebrews 11:31)*

The last person we would expect to find in a list
of Bible heroes is a woman with a checkered
past. Rahab had three strikes against her. First, she
was a Gentile long before Israel took seriously its
command to be a light to the Gentiles. The name of
the Lord did not exist among her people, much less
the knowledge of how to know Him. Second, she
lived in a city God considered too sinful to salvage.
Not only had God ordered Joshua and the armies of
Israel to destroy Jericho; He declared it was never
to be rebuilt. Joshua pronounced this curse after its
destruction: "Cursed before the Lord is the man
who undertakes to rebuild this city, Jericho: At the
cost of his firstborn son will he lay its foundations;
at the cost of his youngest will he set up its gates"
(Joshua 6:26). This was the place Rahab called
home. Finally, Rahab was a prostitute in a culture
known for its sexual decadence. Prostitution
formed a vital part of Baal worship; worshipers
tried to invoke Baal's blessing through fertility rites.
No, Rahab isn't the sort of person we would expect
to find alongside such giants of the faith as Abraham, Joseph, and Moses.

Yet the writer of the book of Hebrews includes her on his list of the faith hall of fame. By faith Rahab welcomed the men from Israel who had come to spy out the land of Canaan. Word of the God who had parted the Red Sea and destroyed Pharaoh's army had spread to Jericho long before the spies arrived. Rahab believed in Him and her life was spared. The second chapter of the book of James sets her alongside Abraham as an example of faith expressing itself in action (vv. 20–26). Rahab does more than tell us about the nature of faith; she shows us the only thing we can hope for when we turn to God, which is His grace. Her name has the unusual meaning of "wide," a term used to describe large fields or a town square. In her case it is the perfect name to describe the breadth of God's mercy and grace.

Rahab's name and her story assure us that no one is beyond forgiveness. We need to be reminded of this on a regular basis. I don't really want to admit this, but one of my greatest obstacles to sharing the gospel is my natural urge to judge others. I think this is something we all carry around deep down inside of us. The sin of others disgusts us, especially those we catalog as *major* sins. You know the ones, sins like murder, rape, child molesting, homosexuality, sexual deviation, abortion. We may say that we love the sinner but hate the sin, yet in the real world the two are hard to separate.

Several years ago I visited the prison in Chino, California, as part of the Bill Glass evangelistic team. I was selected with a handful of other men to go into the HIV isolation unit to give the gospel to the inmates confined to this area. As we walked in, one particular inmate caught the attention of all of us. We probably looked like fools, because our jaws dropped simultaneously in shock and disbelief. This inmate, seated at a center table in the cafeteria, looked like he belonged in the women's facility. From his hair to his fingernails, he was the most effeminate male I had ever encountered. My first (and lasting) impression was to stay as far away from this individual as possible. Most of my fellow counselors made the same decision. Finally, one man from our group walked over to this individual, shook his hand, and sat down to eat and discuss the gospel with him. Only then did I realize how my judgmental spirit separated this man from the good news he desperately needed to hear.

I'm glad that God isn't as harsh with sinners as I find myself wanting to be. If He were, I wouldn't be writing these words right now. I'd still be stuck in a dead-end lifestyle of anger and bitterness. It is all too easy for us to forget how disgusting our sin is in the eyes of God. You and I are no different from a prostitute in Jericho or an inmate in Chino. We all have sinned, every one of us, and God's grace is great enough to forgive us all. This is the beauty of Rahab's story. She assures us that everyone, no matter what he or she has done, *can* be forgiven because of the greatness of God's grace, while also reminding us that everyone, no matter what he or she has (or hasn't) done, *must* find forgiveness in God's grace.

In Rahab we see how God's grace spreads beyond forgiveness to acceptance into His family. After her life was spared by Joshua's invading army, Rahab became a part of the nation of Israel. With time she apparently married a member of the tribe of Judah and gave birth to a son named Boaz. Boaz married Ruth, who had a son named Obed. Obed was the father of Jesse, and Jesse was the father of David, king of Israel. A thousand years later Mary, another descendant of Rahab, had a son. His name was Jesus. When a peanut farmer from Georgia became president, we said, "Only in America." When a prostitute becomes a part of the family tree of the Savior of the world, we can only shake our heads and say, "Only by the grace of God."

This really should not surprise us. God delights in choosing unlikely people to be part of His family. He doesn't look for the best and the brightest; instead He calls people like you and me. The references on our résumés don't impress Him, and the long list of failures we try to hide doesn't cause Him to look for someone else. He likes finding someone like Rahab, someone in desperate need of His grace, so that He can show the greatness of His mercy through her to all of creation.

The church in Corinth forgot this truth. For some reason their opinion of themselves became inflated. Paul brought them back down to earth when he reminded them that the vast majority of them were not wise by human standards or of noble birth. Christianity hadn't yet become the respectable religion of the upper middle class. Rather, the church of Corinth was made up of people like Rahab—former adulterers, prostitutes, homosexuals, thieves, drunkards, swindlers, greedy people (1 Corinthians 6:9–11). In the light of God's grace, it doesn't matter what we used to be. All that matters in God's eyes is what we are through Christ and what we will be. He doesn't concentrate on our past. Instead He focuses us on what we will become through His grace.

We need to learn one final lesson from the life of Rahab. She played a vital role in the success of the children of Israel's conquest of the land of Canaan. Jericho was the oldest and one of the most important cities in the region. Its strategic location dictated that it be conquered first. For this reason Joshua sent two spies to look over the land, especially the city of Jericho. But they were found out. Word came to the king of Jericho that the spies were in the city, and he began a manhunt for them. His search took him to the home of Rahab. Rather than turn the men over to the king to be killed, she hid them under piles of flax and helped them escape to the hills. She risked her life for these two strangers because she was convinced that "the Lord your God is God in heaven above and on the earth below" (Joshua 2:11).

I'm sure the Lord could have found someone more reputable than Rahab to preserve the mission of the spies, but that is not how He operates. He loves to show the magnitude of His grace by transforming real live sinners into integral parts of His operations on planet Earth.

Few people were as powerful in the early seventies as a forty-year-old chief adviser to the president. He was the second most important man in the nation, second only to the president himself. But only after Charles Colson, Nixon's hatchet man, fell from power and became a convicted Watergate co-conspirator did God's ultimate plan for his life begin to unfold. The Lord didn't have much use for a Washington power broker; He could do much more through a convicted felon and former prison inmate.

I find it amazing how God turns our past failures into avenues for ministry today. When His grace sets us free from sin, it turns us loose to begin changing the lives of others. The very sins that brought us so much shame before we came to Christ open new doors for us to minister to people suffering through similar experiences. Charles Colson's time in a federal prison resulted in the creation of Prison Fellowship, a worldwide ministry touching the lives of prisoners, their families, and their victims. Only a very big God could pull off something like this, and only a vast amount of grace can bring it down to you and me.

Let me sound one word of caution at this point: We must be careful not to take the greatness of God's grace for granted. A very real danger exists that we will become so accustomed to His forgiveness that we stop taking sin seriously. A recent phone call I received drove this truth home to me. An old friend, a fellow pastor, called me the other day. When I asked how he was, he simply said, "I'm single." This came as a shock since he and his wife had been married more than twenty-five years. My first thought was that his wife was dead. No, he assured me, she wasn't dead, only their marriage was. He left her and the ministry for another woman. The divorce is permanent, he assured me, but his time out of the ministry is not. Now, he said, he will be able to better relate to his parishioners who go through the pain of divorce, since he has experienced it himself. For my friend, the grace of God has become nothing more than a license to sin.

We have to guard ourselves against this idea. God's grace is as vast as the sea. Our minds can never comprehend its greatness. But He shows us mercy to rescue us from sin, not to give us an excuse to continue living in it. From the day Joshua spared Rahab her life changed. When God's grace touches our lives, our lives will change too.

God, break the judgmental streak that runs through my heart. Open my eyes to see people the way You do. So often my judgmental heart is nothing more than a shield to try to hide my own sin. Break me; set me free. Transform the failures I am so ashamed of into avenues You can use to change lives. Amen.

And what more shall I say? I do not have time to tell about Gideon, Barak, Samson, Jephthah, David, Samuel and the prophets, who through faith conquered kingdoms, administered justice, and gained what was promised; who shut the mouths of lions, quenched the fury of the flames, and escaped the edge of the sword; whose weakness was turned to strength; and who became powerful in battle and routed foreign armies. Women received back their dead, raised to life again. *(Hebrews 11:32–35)*

13

GIDEON
One who cuts to pieces

Gideon said to God, "If you will save Israel by my hand as you have promised— look, I will place a wool fleece on the threshing floor. If there is dew only on the fleece and all the ground is dry, then I will know that you will save Israel by my hand, as you said." And that is what happened. Gideon rose early the next day; he squeezed the fleece and wrung out the dew—a bowlful of water. *(Judges 6:36–38)*

One of Jesus' most famous sayings is also one of his most puzzling. His disciples requested of Him, "Lord, increase our faith!" Listen to His response, "If you have faith as small as a mustard seed, you can say to this mulberry tree, 'Be uprooted and planted in the sea,' and it will obey you" (Luke 17:6). Since the day He uttered those words, people have wondered what exactly He was talking about. On another occasion He said that faith like a mustard seed can move mountains. Interpreters look at mulberry trees and mountains metaphorically to speak of the great obstacles we will face in the Christian life.

What I find puzzling is the fact that I've never seen any trees uprooted by faith, nor have I ever met someone who could command one of the Sierra Nevada mountains (or even an Indiana hill) to get up and move. Jesus' point wasn't to give us an alternative to bulldozers. Rather, He was assuring us that it doesn't take much faith to both please Him and do great works for Him.

Gideon found this to be true long before Jesus walked on the earth. We remember him as God's horn blower and the man with the fleece. In many ways his faith was the size of a mustard seed. He became frightened in the face of opposition, he questioned God when the Lord told him to do something, and he asked for tangible proof of God's will before he would act. Gideon alters our view of what it means to walk by faith by bringing it down to our level. Reading through his life story, which is found in Judges chapters six through eight, I find myself saying, "Wow, he's like me; he does that too." His example is far from perfect. In Gideon we find the answer to the question of how much faith it takes for God to use us. Apparently, we only need about as much as a mustard seed.

God first spoke to Gideon during a desperate time in Israel's history. In the book of Judges, every time was a desperate time. In the days before a king, Israel went through a repetitive cycle. The people would turn away from the Lord; He would send judgment through one of the surrounding nations; the Israelites would turn back to Him, crying out for help; and God would send a deliverer, a judge. A few years after the deliverer's death the cycle would repeat itself. On this particular occasion, things were so bad that the Israelites abandoned their homes and hid in caves from the oppression of the Midianites. Bands of raiders would sweep into Israel on camels, destroying crops and driving away herds. When the Angel of the Lord found

Gideon, he was threshing wheat in a winepress to escape detection by the Midianites.

When the Angel of the Lord appeared to Gideon, He called out, "The Lord is with you, mighty warrior" (Judges 6:12).

"If the Lord is with us," Gideon replied, "why are all these bad things happening? It looks like He has abandoned us. Where are all the wonders we hear in the old stories of the time God delivered our fathers from Egypt?" (see v. 13).

The Lord's next line came as a complete shock. "Go in the strength you have and save Israel out of Midian's hand. Am I not sending you?" (Judges 6:14).

"You're sending who . . . me? . . . Are You talking to me? Now wait a minute, God, uh . . . how can I save Israel? . . . Don't You know who I am? My clan, it's the weakest in all of Israel, and me . . . I am the least in my family. No, You don't want me, do You?" These were not Gideon's exact words, but they would be mine. *Maybe You have a wrong number, God. You didn't mean to call me—surely You meant to call someone else.* I find that I become intimidated by a lot less than it took to scare Gideon. So do most of the people I know. Our palms become clammy and we break out in a cold sweat at the thought of teaching a fourth-grade boys' Sunday school class. It's a good thing the Midianites don't live anywhere near us.

Gideon's reaction, and ours, could be called a lack of faith, but the rest of his story reveals that he did not doubt God's ability to drive out the Midianites. He wondered why God would choose *him*. What did he have to offer God? Most of us share his

apprehension. We know that God can do anything
and everything He sets His mind to. Stories of His
doing the impossible don't surprise us. We know
there's nothing our God cannot do. That is, until He
drops us into the middle of the work He wants to
do. Suddenly everything changes. It is not that we
now doubt God. We wonder why He would choose
us. For some reason we have a very hard time seeing ourselves in the stories we hear others tell of
how God works through human beings to do the
miraculous. Gideon probably loved the story of
Joshua and the battle of Jericho, but he never imagined he would someday be the one leading Israel's
army into an impossible battle. Faith doesn't neces-
sarily mean jumping immediately at the opportunities God presents to us. Instead, it takes us
through our doubts and causes us to cast ourselves
on God as our only hope of success.

We usually do what Gideon did: We ask for
some tangible proof of God's plan. Three times
Gideon requested a sign from God, and three times
God complied. The first sign came before his first
covert operation. The Lord instructed Gideon to
cut down the Asherah pole his family used in order
to seek favor from the pagan gods of the Canaanites. This would be comparable to a Mormon
throwing out all of his family's LDS material. Before
he complied Gideon asked for a sign. He brought
out bread and meat, and the Lord touched it and
burned it up.

The second and third signs came together. God
challenged Gideon with a mission so large, so impossible, that he wanted to make doubly sure
before he set out. He was instructed to attack the

combined forces of the Midianites, Amalekites, and other Eastern peoples—an army so large that they were as thick as locusts in the valley of Jezreel. All the fighting men in all the tribes of Israel paled in comparison. Gideon sounded his trumpet and called the tribes of Manasseh, Asher, Zebulun, and Naphtali to arms. Then, before they marched into battle, Gideon fell on his knees with a simple request of God: "If you will save Israel by my hand as you have promised, cause the dew to cover this fleece while the surrounding ground stays dry" (see Judges 6:36). The next day, after God did precisely what Gideon had asked, he repeated his request, reversing the order by asking that the fleece stay dry while the ground be soaked with dew. Once again, God complied.

Throwing out fleeces is not the best way to discern the will of God. Gideon already had God's plan for his life. The signs confirmed what he already knew. Once Gideon knew for certain that God was calling him to do something, he did it with all his might. I don't know many people willing to take such an unpopular stand as destroying the regional idol to the dominant false religion. Nor do I know many people anxious to go into battle with an army of three hundred men against one hundred twenty thousand. The writer of the book of Hebrews puts Gideon alongside the other heroes of the Bible because he did both of these, in spite of his fear, in spite of his uncertainty about himself.

All of us want some sort of proof that faith works before we are willing to commit ourselves to it. We want to hear the testimonies of others, or we want to see some sort of tangible proof of the will of

God. Problems arise when we become stuck at the point of the sign, when we never take the step of faith and follow the Lord in obedience. Gideon asked for two signs with fleeces, but then he went out to war for God. Some of us get stuck with the fleece. We throw it out to God, He answers, we throw it out again, He answers, we throw it out again . . . The problem we often face is not one of needing assurance of God's will, but of our unwillingness to do what God shows us to do.

The need for tangible proof of God's will comes early in our pilgrimage of faith. We believe, but we just need a little help from God with our unbelief. Our faith must grow beyond this point. With time we must learn to discern the will of God and do it. God doesn't always answer our requests for signs. Mature faith goes forward without physical evidence that God will do what He promised.

Few people in the Bible fought a battle as spectacular as the one Gideon led Israel's armies into. He marched out toward Jezreel with a force of thirty-two thousand fighting men. Before they reached Midian's camp the Lord whittled that force down to three hundred men. As God told Gideon to reduce the men in his command, Gideon obeyed without asking questions, without asking for a sign. He was still frightened, he still wondered how on earth three hundred men could ever defeat one hundred twenty thousand; but in spite of his fear and apprehension he obeyed. And God gave him the victory. Gideon's faith looks rather small at first glance. There wasn't much to it. But that was all God needed to work through Gideon to bring glory to Himself.

You don't have to be a faith giant to be usable to God. Nor do you need to be a fearless spiritual warrior. All you need is the faith that believes that God can do the impossible and the willingness to let Him prove that through you. A mustard seed's worth of faith, that is all you or I need to be used by God.

What a relief, Lord; You really meant it when You said we only need faith the size of a mustard seed. Praise You, O Father, for Your marvelous grace. Thank You for not rejecting me during my times of doubt. Strengthen my faith, and wean me away from signs, that I might go forward into the unknown with You. Amen.

14

BARAK

Thunderbolt, the Lord's flashing sword

Then Deborah said to Barak, "Go! This is the day the Lord has given Sisera into your hands. Has not the Lord gone ahead of you?" So Barak went down Mount Tabor, followed by ten thousand men. At Barak's advance, the Lord routed Sisera and all his chariots and army by the sword, and Sisera abandoned his chariot and fled on foot. *(Judges 4:14–15)*

I love the meaning of Barak's name. Thunderbolt. Someone with a name like this belongs on the "American Gladiators" TV show alongside Nitro and Zap. His name alone tells you that this is one character you don't want to mess with. Barak's dad must have had big plans for his son to give him the name of "the Lord's flashing sword." He was a superstar in the making, a man born to be a fighter. Barak lived up to his name; he was a mighty warrior for God. With ten thousand foot soldiers he led the charge against the iron chariots of Sisera, the Canaanite general. At Barak's advance, the Lord routed the Canaanites, and their entire army was destroyed. God's thunderbolt not only fought in the battle; he led the charge down Mount Tabor and pursued his enemies until they were totally annihilated. His exploits made him ancient Israel's Teddy Roosevelt or General Patton, a great military leader who never shrunk back in the face of danger.

It seems odd then to find Barak in the shadow

of others, especially in the shadow of two women. He did not lead Israel; God gave that responsibility to Deborah. Nor did he receive the glory from his greatest military expedition. Jael, the wife of Heber the Kenite, struck the decisive blow by killing the commander of the oppressing army. Barak led the charge against the supreme military weaponry of his day, and he risked his life to deliver Israel from twenty years of oppression, but someone else received the glory. When we see his name in the eleventh chapter of Hebrews we wonder who he is. Thunderbolt, the Lord's flashing sword, is little more than a Bible trivia question for most of us. People who dwell in the shadows tend to be forgotten.

Maybe that is why almost all of us are so often overlooked. We live in the shadows. Life doesn't have room for many superstars. Our jobs blend us in with the rest of our co-workers, and we become lost in the shadow of the product our factory produces or of the corporate spokesman. We live anonymously in our cities and neighborhoods. Outside a small circle of family and friends, no one knows who we are. The president doesn't make a point of dropping by our house for dinner when he is in town. Even at church most of us don't stand out. There's always someone more visible, someone who receives the honor as if he worked alone, even though we are a vital part of his success. We live our lives lost in the crowd, working in the shadows of others.

Frankly, I find myself resenting this. Deep down inside, all of us want to be recognized for what we do. We want people to notice us. When I was eight years old, I played Little League football for the first time. At the end of the season our coach asked us to vote for the most valuable player on our team, as well as the top offensive and defensive players. He gave us ballots and I voted for the one player I thought deserved every award . . . which, I am embarrassed to say, was me. I was a lineman. I blocked so that others could carry the ball to glory, but I thought I deserved the same recognition as our star quarterback. Needless to say, I didn't win any awards, either in that or any other season, but I craved recognition. We all do.

The interesting part of Barak's story is how easily he dwelt in the shadows. After the battle with the Canaanites was won, Deborah and Barak sang a victory song which included this line:

> *In the days of Jael, the roads were abandoned;*
>   *travelers took to winding paths.*
> *Village life in Israel ceased,*
>   *ceased until I, Deborah, arose,*
>   *arose a mother in Israel. (Judges 5:6–7)*

This song firmly placed Deborah in the limelight. She received the honor as the one responsible for leading Israel out of the darkness of judgment and back to the Lord. Barak never complained about Deborah's leadership role or the credit she received. Jael, another woman, killed Sisera, the Canaanite commander, but only after Barak had already routed his army. Jael was praised as the most blessed of women (Judges 5:24). No one called Barak the most blessed of men, even though he was responsible for Israel's victory. Yet he never complained. He never said of Jael, "Sure, she killed one man, but I defeated an army." You don't find those words com-

ing out of Barak's mouth. He gladly accepted his
place in the shadows; he let others bask in the glory
that could have been rightfully his. He surrendered
that right when he hesitated to lead the army as he
had been told to do (Judges 4:8–9), but he accepted the lower place humbly.

Barak learned a lesson every one of us needs to
learn. There is a tremendous freedom and joy that
comes from willingly choosing to take the lowest
place, choosing to be humble. Humility is more
than a spiritual concept. On a practical level, true
humility means working very hard at a task, not re-
ceiving any personal recognition, and rejoicing. It
means living in the shadow of others and not resenting them for it. The Bible has a simple name for
those who choose humility: servants. Servants, or
more accurately slaves, were a common part of
everyday life in the ancient Near East. No one took
the time to praise them for their work. Slaves were
expected to do everything they were told. Once
their work was done their master received the glory.
The cities of Pithom and Rameses in Egypt were
built by Hebrew slaves, but the ruling Pharaoh is
credited with building them. It's not fair, but it was
the way of life for slaves.

As followers of Jesus, you and I are called to
have the attitude of a servant, the same attitude we
see in Jesus:

> *Your attitude should be the same as that of Christ Jesus:*
> *Who, being in very nature God,*
> *did not consider equality with God something to*
>   *be grasped,*
> *but made himself nothing,*

taking the very nature of a servant.
(Philippians 2:5–7)

We're fooling ourselves if we try to confine this attitude to the "spiritual" part of our lives. The heart of a servant needs to flow out of our lives every waking hour, whether we are in the safe confines of our church or in the hostile dog-eat-dog world of business. Servants, by definition, don't crave the spotlight. They don't need the recognition of others to keep going. They work in the shadows, knowing that God recognizes what they do.

The life of Barak gives us the perfect opportunity to explore humility. He shows us how it works in the real world. For a fighting man, a general, it must have been difficult to sit by while crowds praised someone else for his work. It was difficult, but he chose to do just that. I learned this lesson in my first church staff position. Hilltop Baptist Church hired me to be their invisible man . . . I mean the minister of education. No one noticed the work I did, but they noticed when it did not get done. At first this bothered me. I wanted some recognition for the work I did. Soon this began to eat at me and poison my attitude on the job. But then the Lord redirected my attention to the passage in Philippians I referred to a moment ago. He subtly let me know how wrong I was. Then by His grace He taught me the joy of working in the shadows while others enjoy the glory.

Through the years He has had to repeat this lesson several times. I am glad He has done so. Taking on the attitude of a servant is not optional for followers of Jesus Christ. The day we said yes to Je-

sus we signed on to a team where only the Captain
receives praise. We are working for the Lord. Our
goal is to glorify Him. Like John the Baptist, our
motto needs to be, "He must increase, but I must
decrease." Christians are to be mirrors reflecting the
light of the glory of God to men and reflecting the
praises men heap on us to God. The Lord calls us to
lose our lives in the shadow of the Cross. Like
Barak, we fight spiritual battles, and we spend our
entire lives trying to advance the kingdom of God,
but someone else receives the honor. It is our calling; it is the heart of who we are.

Without the attitude of a servant, everything
we do is for naught. Let me repeat that. When we
crave praise and recognition from others, all of our
accomplishments mean nothing on a scale of eternity. Jesus warned His disciples that when people
work for applause, applause will be their only reward, no matter how spectacular their work may
be. Anything done out of selfish ambition means
nothing in the eyes of God.

Barak, the man destined for greatness, is one of
the least known heroes found in the eleventh chapter of Hebrews. I believe the writer chose him for a
definite purpose. His life calls us to become what
few people would want to be: humble servants la-
boring in the shadows of others.

*Make me a servant, O Lord. Crucify my flesh so
that my attitude will reflect the attitude of Your Son
when He walked on the earth. Part of me craves attention, recognition for the work I do. Set me free so that I
can lose my life to advance Your kingdom. Amen.*

15

SAMSON
Of the sun

Then Samson prayed to the Lord, "O Sovereign Lord, remember me. O God, please strengthen me just once more, and let me with one blow get revenge on the Philistines for my two eyes." *(Judges 16:28)*

Few pitchers have ever burst onto the major-league scene like Steve Howe. The 1980 Rookie of the Year with the Los Angeles Dodgers, he was *the* dominant relief pitcher in baseball in the early 1980s. He had a ninety-two-mile-an-hour fastball and an attitude to match. Brash, cocky, and talented, his future was a lock. He was a great pitcher on a team known for producing Hall of Famers like Sandy Koufax and Don Drysdale.

But Steve Howe will never be elected to the Hall of Fame. All of his potential evaporated when his problems with cocaine surfaced. The Dodgers eventually gave up on him, but that did not stop his chemical abuse. For several years teams continued giving him chances, but the story always ended the same way: The drugs and alcohol returned and his career disappeared. He had so much talent that he could have been a real-life Roy Hobbs, a natural, one of the greatest to ever play the game, if he had only stayed away from the things that destroyed his life in baseball. At the time of this writing, Steve Howe continues to work at staying clean and sober. I pray that he is successful.

The names are different, yet the story line is the same for one of the most famous of Israel's judges. Samson overflowed with potential. In one battle, he fought one thousand men and single-handedly defeated them all. With his bare hands he tore down the doorposts of the city gate of Gaza and carried them on his shoulders up a hill. Given his natural abilities and the special anointing God placed upon him, he could have been the greatest leader/warrior in ancient Israel's history. He could have been, but he wasn't. Samson, God's strongman, a man whose name speaks of the spotlight God placed on him, took all of his potential and threw it away. He might have become a true hero of the faith and an example of faithfulness if he had followed God's plan for his life. Instead his life serves as a warning of the dangers of wasting the gifts the Lord places in our lives.

I want to encourage you to take a few moments to turn to the book of Judges and read the story of Samson's life. You can find it in the thirteenth through the sixteenth chapters. His birth was announced by the Angel of the Lord. God made it clear that this was no ordinary child. From the day of his birth Samson was to be a Nazirite, someone set apart to God and His purposes. That meant he could not drink wine, eat anything unclean, or cut his hair. Samson's father and mother sought guidance from the Lord as to how they were to raise this boy. Chapter thirteen of Judges paints a picture of them as faithful servants of the Lord. The Holy Spirit rested on Samson even when he was a child. God blessed him and stirred him to go out and deliver Israel. Based solely on what we read about his birth and childhood, we expect great things out of Samson.

Apparently Samson never took his Nazirite vows, or God, seriously. Anger and his sexual appetite ruled his life. Before his life ended he violated every one of the instructions God gave his parents regarding his Nazirite vow. Overall, there is a complete lack of godly character in Samson. God used him to defeat the Philistines, but He worked in spite of Samson's character, not because of it. The Lord used Samson's bad temper to lash out at the Philistines, but that doesn't mean that the Lord approved of his character. He was a man of great strength and remarkable abilities, yet these were never combined with faith. Only after God had taken everything else away did Samson turn to God. By then it was too late. Everything he could have been, the great impact he could have made on the history of Israel—everything was gone.

I come away from the story of Samson saying to myself, "What a waste." Little boys love to read about his strength, but no parents want their son to grow up to be like him. Samson had everything he could possibly need. As a result he never sought the Lord—he never thought it necessary.

The book of Judges records two of his prayers, neither of which reflects deep devotion to God. His first recorded prayer came after he won a great battle over the Philistines with the jawbone of a donkey. After the battle he became very thirsty. Listen to his prayer: "You have given your servant this great victory. Must I now die of thirst and fall into the hands of the uncircumcised?" (Judges 15:18). Try as I might, it is hard to put a spin on this prayer

that will make it appear to be the heartfelt prayer of
a man who intimately knew the Lord. His second
recorded prayer came at the end of his life. Several
months after his eyes were plucked out, the
Philistines brought him into the temple of Dagon,
where they celebrated the victory their god had giv-
en them. Three thousand men and women were on
the roof watching Samson perform. They praised
Dagon, saying, "Our god has delivered our enemy
into our hands, the one who laid waste our land
and multiplied our slain" (Judges 16:24). When
Samson cried out to the Lord he did not ask that
God's name be avenged over the god of the Philistines.
Instead he asked for revenge for his eyes. It was
about as humble as Samson could be. And God
gave him the strength to bring down the temple
and thereby kill all the pagan worshipers at his own
death.

The tragedy of Samson's life is what could have
been. Can you imagine what his life would have
been like if his natural abilities were combined with
David's passion for God? How different the life of
Israel would have been during this time if Samson
had copied Samuel's firm stand for the law of God.
Samson's life is filled with "could haves" and
"should haves," wasted potential.

You and I need to listen closely to the story of
Samson because we have a lot in common with
him. We, like Samson, have everything we can possibly need. Times may come where we have to
depend upon God for everything and if He doesn't
come through we will not survive, but most of us
live in relative comfort. Our prosperity leads to an
anemic faith. God becomes the god of the gaps, fill-

ing in what all of our material goods cannot supply. Rather than being our all in all, our strength and our shield, He becomes an afterthought, Someone we turn to in times of crisis. Samson desperately sought the Lord when he was thirsty, but when the water flowed, his faith was washed away. After our crises end, we too have the tendency to go back to our old ways of life until the next crisis strikes.

Together we also share Samson's great potential. Can you imagine the impact the church could make on our world if those who know the Lord would give their all to the kingdom of God? The possibilities are endless. Just think of how quickly the gospel would spread around the world if each believer of Jesus Christ committed himself to reaching one person with the gospel each year. Instead the church treads water. Growth comes as people wander from church to church; very few unconvinced adults are reached. Like Samson, American believers have the potential to radically transform our world, but, like Samson, that potential slips by unfulfilled. The chapters in the book of Judges immediately following the story of Samson describe life in Israel during this period. Be careful about letting your children read these tales, because these stories are more graphic than the nightly news. Why was Israel in such dire straits? Part of the problem came from its yo-yo cycle of devotion to God. I believe the writer of the book of Judges arranged the chapters in this way to show us how bad a nation can become when its spiritual leaders do not take God seriously.

Finally, this tragic story sounds a warning we must heed. The writer of the book of Hebrews includes Samson's name because he did act in faith . . . after he lost everything else. When his strength was gone and his eyes plucked out, when he was no longer the hero of Israel but the laughingstock of the Philistines, then and only then did he cry out, "O Sovereign Lord . . ." The writer of the book of Hebrews groups Samson with others "whose weakness was turned to strength." The tragedy of his life is that his great strength had to be turned to weakness before God could turn his weakness to strength.

Don't fall into Samson's trap. This may sound like an appeal to non-Christians to turn to God before their lives hit bottom, but I know that most of my readers are already believers. We are the ones who must be careful to continually walk by faith, to continually seek the Lord and depend on Him. Samson did not do this. Several times the Scripture says that the Spirit of the Lord came on Samson with power, but we never find him seeking the Lord with his whole heart. God mercifully knocked out all of the props Samson used to keep his life together so that he would finally turn to the One who sought him. We can avoid this painful process by willingly throwing the props away and seeking God now. Samson's story could have had a happy ending, but it is too late for him. Let's not repeat his mistake.

O Lord, protect me from repeating the tragic mistake of Samson. Bind my heart to Yours. O Father, I would rather have nothing in this world and depend on You than to have everything else my heart desires without You. Take my life, and cultivate the potential You have placed in me for Your glory. Amen.

16

JEPHTHAH
He will open

Then the Spirit of the Lord came upon Jephthah. He crossed Gilead and Manasseh, passed through Mizpah of Gilead, and from there he advanced against the Ammonites. And Jephthah made a vow to the Lord: "If you give the Ammonites into my hands, whatever comes out of the door of my house to meet me when I return in triumph from the Ammonites will be the Lord's, and I will sacrifice it as a burnt offering." *(Judges 11:29–31)*

We can learn from everything in the Bible. Every story, every law, every psalm, every promise, every proverb—all of it comes to us as a gift from our Lord so that we can know Him and walk with Him. Books like Proverbs, James, and Philippians are easy to read and easy to apply to our lives. Many of the historic sections inspire us. Tales of Daniel in the lions' den or Shadrach, Meshach, and Abednego in the fiery furnace fill our hearts with resolve to take a bold stand for the Lord. We grow up reading these stories over and over until we know every detail by heart.

But most of us don't know the details of Jephthah's life, even though his name is found on the list of great heroes of the faith in the eleventh chapter of Hebrews. Once we read the account of his life found in the eleventh and twelfth chapters of the book of Judges we understand why he is not very well known. His life puzzles us. We aren't quite sure how to take him. On the day he sets out by faith against impossible odds, he also makes an incredibly foolish vow that makes us wonder if he knew anything at all about God. Fearless, foolish, full of faith, full of inconsistency, he is hard to understand, a fascinating character.

Before we plunge into the life story of Jephthah I need to remind you that the Bible reports the lives of Bible characters without endorsing everything they did. When Scripture reports that men like David and Solomon multiplied wives for themselves, the Lord is not telling us to go and do likewise. People in the Bible are just people, fallen human beings. The Holy Spirit presents a realistic picture of them, complete with warts. The Word of God tells the true stories of real people, not fairy tales about larger-than-life heroes.

Jephthah lived in the period between Joshua and Samuel, the time of the judges. His father was Gilead, a respected member of the tribe of Manasseh, but his mother was a prostitute. Gilead's other sons drove Jephthah away from the family lands, making him an outcast, a traveling warrior with his band of fighting men. Early in his lifetime the tribes of Israel turned away from the Lord . . . again. They copied the surrounding nations and adopted Baal worship, as they had done time after time after time before. And, just as He had done many times before, God punished them through one of their neighbors until they turned back to Him. For eighteen years the Ammonites oppressed the Israelites on the east side of the Jordan. When the Ammonites turned their attention west and began to attack the tribes of Ephraim, Judah, and Benjamin, the Israelites returned to the Lord. They cried out for forgiveness and began to look for a deliverer. God raised up the outcast they had driven away.

The sons of Gilead told Jephthah that he was no good, that he did not deserve to live among them. A few years later God used him to deliver the entire nation. The Lord opened all the doors other people had slammed shut and raised up another unlikely hero. I like this part of the story. It inspires all of us who have ever been told we will never amount to anything. God ignores other people's assessment of our worth. He looks beyond our abilities, inabilities, past failures, and less-than-perfect family histories to see the potential that He planted inside us when He made us. Image may mean everything on Madison Avenue, but it means nothing to our Lord. Sons of prostitutes, outcasts, those whom society looks down their noses on are the very ones God delights to use to do His greatest works. We don't need a sparkling résumé; all we need is faith in God.

The writer of Hebrews included Jephthah in the hall of fame of faith for good reason. He took a bold stand for the Lord in an hour when everyone else cowered in fear. Compromise was never an option for him when the Lord's reputation among the nations was on the line. After eighteen years of oppressing the Israelites, the Ammonite king finally told Israel his terms for peace. He would withdraw his forces in exchange for the return of all of Israel's territory on the east bank of the Jordan River, land occupied by the tribes of Reuben, Gad, and Manasseh. Listen to Jephthah's response:

Now since the Lord, the God of Israel, has driven the Amorites out before His people Israel [and given them this land], what right have you to take it over? Will you not take what your god Chemosh gives you? Likewise, whatever the Lord our God has given us, we will possess. (Judges 11:23–24)

In other words, Jephthah declares, "The Lord God gave us this land and we will not give it back." The territory Israel possessed was more than hills and valley, more than land—it was their inheritance from the Lord. Their presence in this region was a testimony of the power of the God of Abraham, Isaac, and Jacob. He had promised the land to them hundreds of years before, then declared that He alone is God by delivering on His promise. By faith Jephthah told the Ammonites, "We will not budge. God gave us this land. He will not abandon us now." He understood that the battles Israel fought against their enemies were in reality showdowns between rival gods and the one true God. Israel would triumph because their God was real.

Jephthah's stand illustrates the definition of faith we found at the beginning of Hebrews 11. He was sure of what he hoped for, certain of what he did not see. Eighteen years of oppression certainly did not bolster anyone's confidence that the Lord was in control. But Jephthah knew He was. He knew that the One who conquered Egypt, split the Red Sea, and gave Israel the land of Canaan would not turn His back on them now.

We've heard this theme over and over again in the lives of those profiled in the faith chapter. Without faith it is impossible to please God, whereas with faith God does the impossible through those

who please Him. By faith Jephthah conquered the
Ammonites; by faith Rahab hid the spies; by faith
Moses' parents placed him in a floating basket; by
faith Noah built an ark—by faith, by faith, by faith.
These words are used over and over in the hope
that this truth will eventually sink through our
thick skulls. If we are serious about this thing called
Christianity, we must learn to live by faith. Trials
blindside us, and we persevere through them by
faith. God gives us a job to do, and by faith we will
be able to complete it. Life becomes a long, hard
exercise in endurance, but by faith we go through it
with joy. Our own personal Ammonites try to make
our lives miserable, but by faith we cling to Christ
because we know He will never abandon us. By
faith we persevere, by faith we overcome, by faith
we live victoriously.

If it were up to me, the story of Jephthah
would end here. By faith he conquered the Ammonites, then he returned home to lead Israel into
a closer walk with God. Everyone would live happily ever after, and the screen would fade to black.
The end. For some strange reason God didn't leave
the ending of the story up to me. He made sure every
detail was written down, including an episode I
would rather ignore. Shortly before engaging the
Ammonites in battle, Jephthah made a vow to God:
"If you give the Ammonites into my hands, whatever comes out of the door of my house to meet me
when I return in triumph from the Ammonites will
be the Lord's, and I will sacrifice it as a burnt offering" (Judges 11:30–31). I'm not sure what he
expected to walk out of the door of his house.
Maybe the family goat usually ran out to greet him

like an overeager cocker spaniel. Whatever he expected, when he returned home the first thing out of his front door was his daughter, an only child. The Scripture suggests that he followed through with his vow and offered his daughter as a burnt offering.

Some commentators try to make this story more palatable by asserting that he gave his daughter to the Lord by dedicating her to serve at the Tent of Meeting, rather than actually taking her life. However, all of the evidence points to a literal fulfillment of the vow. He offered her as a burnt offering. The thought is repulsive, but true.

Did God honor Jephthah's vow and approve of the human sacrifice? Of course not. Jephthah did not need to make some wild promise on the eve of battle to secure God's favor. All he needed was faith. He couldn't add anything else. Apparently his understanding of who God is and what He requires was incomplete. His vow reflects a superstitious view of God, closer to the theology of the pagan nations than the law of Moses. If he knew the law, he would have also known that he could offer a ransom payment to redeem the life of his daughter. The twenty-seventh chapter of the book of Leviticus says that an adult female dedicated to the Lord by a vow could be redeemed for thirty shekels of silver. If she was age five to twenty (the probable age of this young woman, since she was single), the price of redemption was only ten shekels of silver. All of the evidence indicates that Jephthah never considered this to be an option. Either he did not know the law, or his pride kept him from backing down from his word. In the end, his great victory was turned to intense sorrow as his only child died as a result of the needless vow he made.

How could God use a man like this? And why on earth would he be listed alongside Moses and Abraham as a great hero of the faith? In all honesty I have to admit that I wonder that myself. Perhaps part of the reason God included Jephthah's story is to remind us that God uses imperfect people. I know this sounds like a gross understatement (which it is), but I don't know how else to put it. God works through people who have obvious flaws in their character. I don't know how or why the righteous, holy Lord would use a man like Jephthah, but I also don't know how or why God would use a man like Moses, a man who secretly killed another man. And I don't know how or why God would use a man like Abraham who had a tendency to bend the truth for his advantage. Nor do I know how or why God would use a man like Solomon with his one thousand wives. And, to be quite honest, I don't know how or why God would use a man like me . . . or a person like you. If the Lord required perfection, none of us would stand a chance.

Imperfection is one thing, but to offer your only child as a sacrifice . . . come on, none of us would do something like that. I'm sure that is true. No one in his right mind would physically sacrifice his child, but how many of us sacrifice just as much on the altar of success? Jephthah's act may be atrocious to our eyes, but much of what we do is equally repulsive to God. Just because God blesses your life or uses you in some way for His kingdom does not mean that God endorses everything you do. Martin Luther stands out as a hero to many of us. We admire his bold stand of faith. His words still ring in our ears, "Here I stand, I can do no other . . . " Awe inspiring—there is no other word for him. But the same man who was the spark plug for the Protestant Reformation was also anti-Semitic. The same man who said, "Here I stand," also said that Jews were lazy leeches on society. Does the fact that God did so much through Luther mean that our Lord hates Jews as well? The whole history of Scripture says otherwise.

Success, especially spiritual success, has a way of blinding us to our flaws. God may use you to lead your neighbors to Christ, but that does not mean that He has decided to overlook the secret sin you harbor deep inside. The fact that God uses you and me does not mean He endorses everything we do. I find this truth to be humbling and chilling. Jephthah's tragic end reminds us that we must constantly measure ourselves against the standard of Scripture and strive to walk humbly with our God.

Lord, open my eyes to the secret sins I harbor deep inside, sins I don't think You notice since You continue to shower Your blessings upon me. Jephthah's vow shocks and disgusts me; I don't want to think about how much I am like him. Deliver me from my secret sins; deliver me from my foolishness. I want to walk humbly and in a holy manner before You. Amen.

17

DAVID
Favorite, beloved

> After removing Saul, [God] made David their king. He testified concerning him: "I have found David son of Jesse a man after my own heart; he will do everything I want him to do." (*Acts 13:22*)

I'm struggling as I attempt to write this chapter. It deals with sin, a subject I would rather ignore. Even that last sentence doesn't sound quite right. I wish I could ignore sin and have nothing to do with it, like I ignore the kitchen trash can when it overflows. But I don't. I like to sin too much. The word *sin* carries so much baggage, all of it bad and negative. I prefer to speak of my weaknesses or shortcomings. Rather than think of myself as a sinner, I like to categorize myself as someone who is less than perfect but striving to do my best. That sounds better. It gives me an air of respectability, as if my occasional missteps are not my fault.

But I don't always strive to do my best, and my missteps are more than temporary lapses into imperfection. They are sin. And not just sin in a general sense, but specific acts that I know are wrong. I try to ignore them or to gloss over their seriousness, and I do a good job. That is, I succeed until I begin to study the life of a man like David. He was a man after God's own heart, yet he committed horrible acts deserving of death. God did not abandon him, nor did He overlook what he had done. David's story brings all of my games with God concerning my sin crashing down around me, for I cannot speak of faith and forgiveness without wrestling with the way God sees my sin. And that is what makes this chapter so uncomfortable to write, and so necessary.

Using the term "hero" to describe David is an understatement. The writer of the book of Hebrews places him in the list of those he doesn't have the space to write about, and for good reason. Like Moses in the first half, David dominates the latter half of Old Testament history. His exploits fill the books of First and Second Samuel, and the songs he wrote can be found in the book of Psalms. All of the kings of Israel and Judah were measured against the standard he set during his forty-year reign. We think of David as the giant-killer, the man who united Israel and ushered in her golden age. His name describes his character, for he truly was God's favorite, a man after the Lord's own heart.

None of that prevented the tragic turn of events recorded in 2 Samuel 11:2–4, 27:

> *One evening David got up from his bed and walked around on the roof of the palace. From the roof he saw a woman bathing. The woman was very beautiful, and David sent someone to find out about her. The man said, "Isn't this Bathsheba, the daughter of Eliam and the wife of Uriah the Hittite?" Then David sent messengers to get her. She came to him, and he slept with her. (She had purified herself from her uncleanness.) Then she went back home. . . . After the time of mourning was over, David had her brought to his house, and she became his wife and bore him a son. But the thing David had done displeased the Lord.*

David, the man after God's own heart, gave in
to temptation and did the unthinkable. He sent for
another man's wife and slept with her. When she
found that she was pregnant, David tried to cover
his tracks by sending her husband, one of his own
soldiers, to the front lines where he died in battle;
then he married Bathsheba. The hero of the Old
Testament, the poet whose prayers fill the book of
Psalms, committed both adultery and murder. To
say he fell into sin is a gross understatement. According to the law of Moses, both of these acts were
punishable by death. Not only did David commit
them, but he did so with relative ease.

About a year later, the prophet Nathan came to
David with a story:

> There were two men in a certain town, one rich and the
> other poor. The rich man had a very large number of
> sheep and cattle, but the poor man had nothing except
> one little ewe lamb he had bought. He raised it, and it
> grew up with him and his children. It shared his food,
> drank from his cup and even slept in his arms. It was
> like a daughter to him. Now a traveler came to the rich
> man, but the rich man refrained from taking one of his
> own sheep or cattle to prepare a meal for the traveler
> who had come to him. Instead, he took the ewe lamb
> that belonged to the poor man and prepared it for the
> one who had come to him. (2 Samuel 12:1–4)

When he heard the story, David screamed for
justice. He insisted that the guilty man must die . . .
until Nathan told him, "You are the man!" (v. 7). To
a small degree David was made to feel what God
felt when David sinned. Yet the Lord's anger and
disappointment were magnified because He knew

and loved both parties. His anger burned against
the one who would steal another man's wife; His
heart broke at the thought that one He loved would
commit such an act.

Listen to Nathan's words to David as Nathan
spoke for the Lord:

> *I anointed you king over Israel, and I delivered you from
> the hand of Saul. I gave your master's house to you, and
> your master's wives into your arms. I gave you the house
> of Israel and Judah.* And if all this had been too lit-
> tle, I would have given you even more. *Why did
> you despise the word of the Lord by doing what is evil in
> his eyes?* (2 Samuel 12:7–9, emphasis added)

Do you feel the emotion in the Lord's words? "I
gave you everything," He said. "Is this how you re-
pay My kindness?" The Old Testament prophets
used the analogy of a husband whose wife leaves
him to become a prostitute to describe what hap-
pens when God's people sin against Him. That
word picture captures the mixture of heartbreak
and anger God felt when David killed Bathsheba's
husband, and what He feels every time you and I
turn from Him.

Your sin and mine may not be as "big" as
David's, but God's reaction to it is the same. Yes, sin
makes Him angry, but it is an anger filled with grief
and heartbreak. He loves you and me so much that
He sacrificed His Son in order that we might know
Him personally. As if that were not enough, He gives
us His Spirit so that we will never be apart from
Him. When we willfully sin we take everything God
has done for us and trample it underfoot. In effect
we look at the cross and say, "No big deal. God has

to forgive me; it's His job." God doesn't have a hierarchy of vices. Every act of disobedience personally offends our Lord. Every one. We insult the Lord and tarnish His reputation in the world with our actions.

What set David apart, what made him a hero, is how he dealt with his sin after he realized what he had done. Second Samuel 12:13 understates his response when he confessed to Nathan, "I have sinned against the Lord." Listen to the cry for mercy we hear in the psalm he composed for the occasion:

> *Have mercy on me, O God. . . .*
> *Against you, you only, have I sinned*
> *and done what is evil in your sight,*
> *so that you are proved right when you speak,*
> *and justified when you judge. . . .*
> *Hide your face from my sins*
> *and blot out all my iniquity.*
> *Create in me a pure heart, O God,*
> *and renew a steadfast spirit within me.*
> *Do not cast me from your presence*
> *or take your Holy Spirit from me.*
> *Restore to me the joy of your salvation*
> *and grant me a willing spirit, to sustain me. . . .*
> *You do not delight in sacrifice, or I would bring it;*
> *you do not take pleasure in burnt offerings.*
> *The sacrifices of God are a broken spirit;*
> *a broken and contrite heart,*
> *O God, you will not despise.*
> *(Psalm 51:1, 4, 9–12, 16–17)*

Sometimes we have the idea that finding forgiveness is a simple as reciting 1 John 1:9, "If we confess our sins, he is faithful and just and will forgive us our sins and purify us from all unrighteousness." Confess, repent, receive; one, two, three; let life continue. David's words from the fifty-first psalm don't sound like a formula. He cried out for mercy; he pleaded with God to purify his heart. His words show us the true nature of confession when he cried out, "Against you, you only, have I sinned." David's prayer reflected a man genuinely broken over his sin. He found forgiveness, but he never even sought it until his eyes were opened to see his sin from God's perspective.

We don't want to wrestle with our sin. Forgiveness, second chances, they are free gifts from God. True. But in one sense the price is very heavy, and true repentance never comes without deep brokenness. Repentance begins with the attitude that I do not deserve to be forgiven. Period. This is our stumbling block. We are so familiar with the Cross and the business of forgiveness that we somehow have concluded that we deserve it. No one who believes he deserves a second chance will be broken enough to seek it.

David's story has a happy ending. God heard his prayer and blotted out his sin. Within God's forgiveness David found that the Lord still had a plan for his life. He remained king over Israel, devoting his final years to preparing the way for the heir to his throne to build the Lord's temple in Jerusalem. David did not give up on God, nor, mercifully, did God give up on him. David's darkest moment did not undo all that God had accomplished through him in the past, nor did it permanently sever his relationship with the Lord.

However, the judgment God pronounced because of David's actions still came to pass. The child conceived in David and Bathsheba's night of passion died. Further tragedy struck the royal family when David's son Ammon defiled his half sister Tamar, and when Ammon was later killed by another of David's sons, Absalom. As time went by, Absalom overthrew his father and took the throne of Israel, forcing David to flee for his life. Joab, the commanding general of David's army, defied his king's orders and killed Absalom, restoring the kingdom to David. All of these events were set in motion by David himself on the night he noticed Bathsheba from his roof.

God's forgiveness doesn't place a canopy over our heads, protecting us from the consequences of our actions. David reaped a bitter harvest as a direct result of the things he did with Bathsheba. Even though he repented and found forgiveness, those consequences still came. What sets David apart is how he accepted God's judgment as just. He did not complain to God or accuse Him of being unfair. When trials came as a result of his sinful choices, he accepted them and continued to cling to the Lord. While he was fleeing Jerusalem a man named Shimei threw rocks at David, shouting curses at him. Rather than allow his generals to strike down Shimei, David told them, "Leave him alone; let him curse, for perhaps the Lord has told him to" (see 2 Samuel 16:10). We remember David for his faith the day he stood up to Goliath; he showed even more the day he walked silently past Shimei without responding to his curses.

This chapter reminds me of the seriousness of sin in the eyes of God. Deep down inside we hope that if we confess our sin fast enough we will be saved from all of the suffering it brings. David reminds us this is not the case. God isn't being unfair when He allows the consequences of our actions to bring our lives to a screeching halt. Far from it. By doing so the Lord reaffirms His love for us, a love so great that He will do whatever it takes to end our love affair with sin.

Asking for forgiveness sounds so hollow at this point, Lord. Please let me feel a small portion of the pain my sin causes You. Break me of my love affair with disobedience, and forgive me for taking Your grace for granted. Purify my heart by first breaking it over the pain I have caused You. Amen.

18
SAMUEL
God is exalted

> The Lord was with Samuel as he grew up, and he let none of his words fall to the ground. And all Israel from Dan to Beersheba recognized that Samuel was attested as a prophet of the Lord. The Lord continued to appear at Shiloh, and there he revealed himself to Samuel through his word. And Samuel's word came to all Israel. *(1 Samuel 3:19–4:1)*

We've explored many people through the pages of this book. Some have been old friends, whereas others were new acquaintances. None of them was perfect. Some, like Samson, are far less than role models for you and me. Yet each one stands out because of his or her faith. By faith they walked with God, by faith they attempted the impossible, by faith they saw prayers answered and kingdoms fall. They are real heroes, men and women who show us the wonderful possibilities that lie ahead of us when we entrust our lives to God.

One of the people featured in the eleventh chapter of Hebrews stands out as a man I have always looked up to. The story of his life reads like an action novel. He was a man of God at a time when such men were in short supply. Popular opinion did not matter to him. Regardless of the cost, he walked with God and proclaimed His word. A true prophet, his name describes his passion: Samuel, God is exalted. Many words characterize him. Fearless. Faithful. Holy. Unique. Above all, Samuel possessed a holy boldness that enabled him to stand alone for God against an apostate priesthood, a rebellious nation, and a disobedient king. That is what I admire most about Samuel—his boldness. He never backed down from a challenge. His faith kept him from being intimidated by anyone, regardless of the person's position.

We need a few more Samuels in our day. Very few people possess the faithful boldness that characterized his life. Timidity plagues believers today. Studies show that less than 10 percent of us will ever lead another person to Christ. The rest of us want to; we may even long to impact our world for God, but fear paralyzes us. We don't say anything, or we confuse brash arrogance for biblical boldness. I recently heard a news report about a boy preacher in a southern state, a boy who did not have a problem with shyness. Every day before school this ten year old would stand in front of his school building and "preach the gospel." Unfortunately, his idea of preaching was screaming at the top of his lungs, "You're all goin' to HELL!" Needless to say, nobody has been converted under his ministry. He has a form of boldness, but it is a poor imitation of what we find in the life of Samuel.

From the beginning of his life, Samuel shows us that there is much more to the boldness faith produces than the willingness to say unpopular things in the name of God. Samuel lived in a dark age. The book of Judges describes the era as a time when everyone did what was right in his own eyes. No one in Israel feared God; in fact, most people were ignorant of Him and His law. Fighting between tribes was so common that the tribe of Benjamin had been almost exterminated. Idolatry was rampant. During this time words from the Lord were rare: As the writer of Samuel puts it, "there were not many visions" (1 Samuel 3:1). No one spoke for God, and no one sought God.

If the nation was in bad shape, the clergy fared even worse under Eli, the high priest. His two sons used their positions as priests to feed their appetites. They took meat from the altar for their own use and seduced women who served at the entrance to the Tent of the Meeting. Their acts showed total contempt for the Lord and His offerings. God meant nothing to them; the offerings and sacrifices were an avenue for personal gain. In spite of his sons' blasphemous actions, Eli remained silent. He honored his sons above God and did nothing to stop them from profaning the altar and the name of the Lord. Samuel saw all of this firsthand because his mother, Hannah, brought him to Eli when she dedicated him to the Lord.

Samuel stood out as unique in the midst of this rebellious generation without saying a word. Even as a boy he condemned Eli's two sons by his actions. Samuel did not fall in with the crowd; he did not conform to popular opinion. He walked with God. Samuel must have felt tremendous pressure to conform to his age, but he chose to obey God regardless of what anyone else did. Imagine the influence Eli's two sons exerted on him as his "role models" in the home of Eli. Yet he refused to follow their example.

Holy boldness begins with a holy life. Before we can take a stand for God those around us must see Him in our lives. Lines like that last sentence make great "Amen" stops in sermons, but everything changes when we walk out of a church service and into the world. Our culture engulfs us with a system of values, conventional wisdom, and an overall outlook on life that is radically different from the standards God sets for us in His Word. We can talk about "standing firm against the tide," but the human species is a lot like gelatin: We tend to conform to whatever mold we are close to. Willpower and a dogged determination to do the right thing evaporate in an instant under the heat of the pressure to be like everyone else.

That is why Samuel was commended for his faith, not his willpower. By faith he stood his ground because he clung to the Lord. He placed his life in the hands of God and by faith sought refuge there. Even as a boy, there was more to his relationship with the Lord than a commitment to do the right thing. Samuel knew God. Through their intimate times together the Lord's heart became his heart. During Samuel's tenure as Israel's judge, the people came to him demanding a king. Up to this point in Israel's history the nation was essentially a theocracy. Their only king was God Himself. But they wanted to be like all the other nations around them with a national hero to rally around. When Samuel heard their request he got mad, not because the nation rejected him as their judge, but because they rejected God as their king. His heart was so closely tied to God's heart that he felt the same emotions as the Lord. So great was his love for God that he could not bear the thought of someone disgracing His holy name.

We don't usually think of boldness and intimacy with God as related ideas, but we will never have the former without the latter. Look through the pages of the Bible and you will find a common denominator running through the lives of those who took a radical stand for the Lord. All of them consistently pursued an intimate relationship with God. Few people have ever risked as much to pray as Daniel did after Darius issued a decree that everyone in the nation must pray to the king alone. To disobey meant a date with a den of hungry lions. Daniel defied the king, not to take a bold stand against an unjust law, but to spend time with the One he had loved for a lifetime. Peter and John were arrested and brought before the ruling Jewish council under charges of spreading the message of Jesus in the city of Jerusalem. Rather than cower in fear, Peter spoke up and declared that Jesus Christ had risen from the dead. What could give him such boldness when a few weeks earlier he hid in the dark while Jesus was crucified? The council saw the reason. They immediately recognized that these two men had been with Jesus (Acts 4:1–13).

No one wants to be a wimpy, weak-kneed Christian. We read the stories of Daniel and the apostles and we hope that if we ever faced similar circumstances we would take a bold stand for the Lord. Yet we do not realize that every day presents opportunities for us to stand up and be counted with Christ. Until and unless we develop an intimate relationship with the Lord, we will never seize these moments He gives us. Boldness is not a product of personality, but of the Holy Spirit working in our lives. We cannot stir it up within ourselves or

turn it on when we need it. Rather, it flows natural-
ly out of the lives of those who consistently develop
a close relationship with the Lord by faith.

People who know the Lord cannot help but
speak up for Him. Of all the qualities in Samuel's
life, this is the one I admire the most. He spoke for
God regardless of the consequences. It did not matter to him if someone was the high priest or the
king of all Israel: When God gave Samuel a message
he boldly declared all of it. I find that I can talk
straight with someone and say exactly what he
needs to hear when I don't really know the person.
When I sit at a table with a stranger I met only five
minutes before, it is easy for me to tell him he
needs to repent and get right with God. When I sit
at the same table with a close friend or family member, the words tend to get stuck in the back of my
throat.

Samuel talked straight with friends, with people who knew him, with people he worked with
every day. He never stood on a street corner and
screamed at strangers as they passed by. Anyone
can do that. It takes a special individual to sit down
with the man who is raising you and tell him, "You
have upset God with your actions." When he con-
fronted people he wasn't brash or arrogant. Drool
didn't run down his chin while he stomped and
yelled. His actions communicated love and compassion, not hatred and intolerance. When Saul,
Israel's first king, turned from God, the Lord sent
Samuel to confront him. The message he had to tell
was clear: "God has rejected you and has sought
out a man after His own heart to make king" (see
1 Samuel 13:14). But when he spoke this word to

Saul, Samuel didn't go with the demeanor of a television evangelist ranting about the sin of the day. Instead he mourned over Saul. He was heartbroken that the man he had anointed a few years earlier was now rejected by God.

This is true boldness, the kind of boldness that touches other people's lives. Those around us will listen to us when they know we genuinely love them and have their best interest at heart. We can do this. God will implant holy boldness in our lives just as He did in the life of Samuel. The key in Samuel's life was his dedication to God. He surrendered his will to the will of God with nothing held back.

The great need in our world today is not foremost for men and women who will boldly stand where no one has stood before. A much greater need is for men and women who will lose their lives to the will of God. For those people, boldness will follow. From the day of his birth Samuel's entire life was dedicated to the Lord, and it showed in his lifestyle. God set the early church on fire for Him as they lost their lives to Him. Our world needs bold believers who will take a stand for God. You and I can meet that need.

I want to be like Samuel; I want to stand boldly for You, O Lord. Use my life to lift up Your name. When people look at me let them see You instead. Give me the courage to stand and speak for You regardless of the consequences. And let my boldness be filled with Your compassion and love so that lives can be touched through me. Amen.

19

FAITHFUL BUT FORGOTTEN
Destitute, persecuted, mistreated

Others were tortured and refused to be released, so that they might gain a better resurrection. Some faced jeers and flogging, while still others were chained and put in prison. They were stoned; they were sawed in two; they were put to death by the sword. They went about in sheepskins and goatskins, destitute, persecuted and mistreated —the world was not worthy of them. They wandered in deserts and mountains, and in caves and holes in the ground. These were all commended for their faith, yet none of them received what had been promised. *(Hebrews 11:35b–39)*

M ary and Tim had a picture-perfect life. She was a schoolteacher, and he had a good position with a major pharmaceutical company. Both were involved in their local church, and both had a deep love for the Lord. Two bright kids, a nice house, the American dream: God had truly blessed them. But their lives took a dramatic turn downward on a cold November morning when Mary drove down one of the country roads surrounding our small town. A car unexpectedly pulled out in front of her. When she tried to avoid hitting it, her van rolled several times before coming to rest in a soybean field. Paramedics saved her life, but she has not walked since that day. Her neck broke in the accident, paralyzing her body below her shoul-

ders. Was God unfaithful to Tim and Mary, or do
they not have enough faith to raise her from her
wheelchair?

If it weren't for Ron, I might not have ever finished Bible college. He was my typist during my
senior year. But he was more than that; he was one
of my closest friends. Ron completed his master's
degree in theology and also received training in
computer science. Not only does he have a great
theological mind, but he also has a sharp sense of
humor. My wife, Valerie, and I loved to spend time
with Ron and his wife, Pam, during our days in
Dallas. Ron is devoted to his wife, and even more
devoted to his Lord. Ron and Pam now live near
Denver where they are raising their two daughters.
But Ron has never seen his daughters, or his wife,
or me. He has been blind most of his life. Has God
been unfaithful to Ron, or does he not have enough
faith to regain his sight?

Becky was the ultimate grandmother. After
raising eight children of her own, she did everything she could to make the lives of children more
enjoyable. She designed and outfitted the nursery
in our small church so that it was one of the best in
the state of California. Oh, how she loved children.
When I first arrived as her pastor she did her best
to fill the gap that the fifteen hundred miles between Oklahoma City and Springville, California,
created between my children and their grandparents. She had the heart of a servant, and she put
everything she had at the disposal of others. I can't
think of Becky without seeing her gray hair falling
down as she rushed from place to place. Always
moving, always giving. One day her rushing

stopped. Doctors found a spot on her lung. A few months later she was dead from cancer. Was God unfaithful to Becky, or did she not have enough faith to save her life?

The stories could fill volumes. Around the world and throughout time, some of God's most faithful servants are plunged into horrible trials that never end. Some would say that God has turned His back on them, that their lives prove He cannot be trusted. Others would say that the problem lies deep within the persons themselves. If they only had enough faith, their problems would be solved and they would walk out of their trials victorious.

Both statements are completely wrong. God cannot be unfaithful to His promises or His children. And as for a lack of faith on the part of these individuals, consider the case of a missionary whose life story I recently read. Every day he placed his life in precarious situations for the sake of the gospel. He was one of those strange individuals who wanted to go to places where the gospel had never been before, sort of a theological Captain Kirk. Every time he found himself in a scrape, the Lord came through. Somehow he always survived, although the beatings began to take a toll on his body. Finally he found himself in a situation he could not escape. His preaching got him into trouble with the local government. They threw him into prison and sentenced him to death. This wasn't his first time in prison, nor was it his first death sentence, but this time God did not send angels to set him free. The apostle Paul died at the hands of the Roman government. It wasn't his lack of faith that cost him his life—quite the opposite. Paul was so convinced that Jesus is Lord that he refused to be silent, even at the cost of his own life.

Job was also a man of faith, but his great faith did not prevent disaster from striking his home. In one day he suffered the loss of all of his wealth as well as the deaths of his ten children. As if that were not enough, his own health soon failed. His body became so disfigured that his closest friends could not recognize him. I have heard some foolish television preachers declare that Job would not have suffered if he had as much faith as they do. Their assessment of the situation ignores God's statement that "there is no one on earth like [Job]; he is blameless and upright, a man who fears God and shuns evil" (Job 1:8).

Job, Paul, Becky, Ron, Mary, and the saints the writer of Hebrews lists, people whose names history has forgotten, all confront us with the uncomfortable truth that faith does not guarantee a happy, trouble-free life. All of those listed at the close of the eleventh chapter of Hebrews suffered as a direct result of their stand for God. If they had abandoned the faith and turned their back on Christ, all of the misery might have ended. But they refused. They knew what faith was. Faith does not mean believing God for something; it means clinging to God even when we don't have anything else. It means trusting Him and believing His promises even when we never see them come true. Anyone can believe in God when times are good, but individuals are rare indeed who will continue to believe even when their legs don't work, and their eyes don't see, and cancer robs them of life a day at a time. This is what faith is all about.

I have to be honest with you. I don't want to trade places with those so numerous the writer of Hebrews could not list their names. I'm in no hurry to be beaten because I am a Christian or to lose everything I own as a price for following Jesus. Jeers would be bad enough, but floggings? I shudder at the thought. I would much rather be one who had "escaped the edge of the sword" (Hebrews 11:34) than be one of those who were "sawed in two" (v. 37). Wouldn't you? We want a God who overcomes every obstacle, a John Wayne sort of Jesus who always rides in at just the right time to set us free. That kind of god only exists in myths and legends. In the real world faithful people end up in prison for preaching the gospel, and some of them are never released.

The hardest part of thinking about all of this is knowing that "I" could become one of "them" at any moment. Somewhere deep in the recesses of my heart I always think, "Better them than me" when I pray for people in tragic situations. I'll admit it, I do. I thank God that it wasn't my sight that was taken away or my wife who died. But my situation could change at any moment. God does not drop an invisible shield around us when we trust in His Son. He does something even greater. Tragedy may strike, but He never abandons us in the midst of it. He carries us through, even if the journey takes a lifetime. Those who have the greatest faith are those who are willing to trust His faithfulness and cling to Him even if it means their legs will never again support their weight. In spite of the trials, they know that He is Lord, and He is faithful. No wonder the writer of Hebrews says that the world is not worthy of people like this. They live on a different plane than the rest of us. Paul, Job, Becky, Mary, Ron, and those who are like them— they are the true heroes of the faith.

Lord, I don't know what to say in the presence of these of whom the world is not worthy. My flesh hopes that I never go through the pain they've experienced, yet I know that they enjoy a level of fellowship that I can never find surrounded by comfort. Fill my heart with compassion for those who suffer. Strengthen my faith for the day I too will be tested. Amen.

20

YOU AND ME
Saints, holy ones, people set apart to God

These were all commended for their faith, yet none of them received what had been promised. God had planned something better for us so that only together with us would they be made perfect. Therefore, since we are surrounded by such a great cloud of witnesses, let us throw off everything that hinders and the sin that so easily entangles, and let us run with perseverance the race marked out for us. *(Hebrews 11:39–12:1)*

Rugged individualists: This is the essence of what it means to be an American. We are independent. We don't need anyone's help to survive, and neither do our heroes. Like Lewis and Clark traveling across an unexplored continent or Amelia Earhart flying around the world, we can take on any challenge and stand our ground. Moses, the man who took on Pharaoh by himself, would have made a good American. So would Noah, and Gideon, and Samuel. They didn't need anyone else. Their courage and determination gave them the fortitude to face every challenge head-on, to stand their ground when everyone else ran away. That's what we want to be. Brave, courageous, and independent.

But Moses did not stand alone when he uttered his immortal words to Pharaoh, "Let my people go!" Noah did not work alone as he pounded pegs for one hundred twenty years. David was not alone when, armed with nothing but a sling and five stones, he took on Goliath. None of the heroes of the Bible faced their challenges by themselves. Listen to David's words to Goliath as they faced each other in battle, "You come against me with sword and spear and javelin, but I come against you in the name of the Lord Almighty, the God of the armies of Israel, whom you have defied" (1 Samuel 17:45). Obviously, David had God at his side. Every child in a preschool Sunday school class understands that. Yet there is more. Within David's words to Goliath we catch an insight into the way our Old Testament heroes saw themselves in God's plan. All of them understood that they were a part of something much greater than themselves. When David stood in the name of the God of the armies of Israel, he knew that he was a part of those who came before him. In a very real sense, he was not alone. All of the people of God stood alongside him. With this assurance he could single-handedly take on the Philistine champion and prevail.

Not only were these heroes linked to those who came before them, but they are also linked to you and me. As difficult as it is for us to understand, God's eternal plan joins us together with them and all of His people. Apart from us they are incomplete. Apart from them and the rest of God's family, we are incomplete. The idea of the rugged individualist may make a good movie, but it has very little to do with walking by faith. By ourselves we are incomplete. God saves individuals to become a part of His broader family, a family that stretches around the globe and throughout time.

This idea is hard for us to grasp. For one thing, it is difficult to imagine that Abel and Enoch and Sarah spent their entire lives working for something they could never receive in their lifetimes. They were saved, and they are now enjoying heaven's glory, but the one thing upon which they placed their hope in this life was never available to them. God made a promise to them, and they devoted their lives to pursuing it. Yet the promise did not come true until long after their deaths, until the day the One who was promised was born. Now those who looked forward to the coming of Christ and those who live after His resurrection are joined together through the Cross.

Not only are we joined together in the same family in Christ, but those who came before us were serving us through their lives. Listen to Peter's explanation:

> *It was revealed to them [the prophets] that they were not serving themselves but you, when they spoke of the things that have now been told you by those who have preached the gospel to you by the Holy Spirit sent from heaven. Even angels long to look into these things.* (1 Peter 1:12)

Abraham, Isaac, Jacob, David, and Samuel— each one spoke of a promise that was fulfilled long after their brief lifetimes. They would have given anything to know the truths we take for granted. They longed to see the Messiah and to understand how God would once and for all solve the dilemma of sin and forgiveness.

All of this should encourage us. We do not walk alone. The work we attempt for the Lord did not start with us. We're standing on the shoulders

of all those who came before us. None of us has to
start from scratch. Abel did that. He was the first to
walk with God by faith. After he died Seth took up
the baton. Then Enoch, then Noah, then Abraham,
then Isaac, then Jacob. Throughout time the baton
is passed from generation to generation. Each one
who grabs the baton is dependent on the faithfulness of those who ran before, and those who hand
off the baton are dependent on the faithfulness of
those who will continue the race. Although we are
separated by thousands of years and thousands of
miles, we are working together with all of God's
people to reach goals that will last throughout eternity. We may feel alone as we take our turn around
the track, but we are not. The God of Abraham,
Isaac, and Jacob runs with us, as do all of those
who came before us.

    The baton has been passed. Now it is up to you
and me to run our leg of the race. All of those who
have run before now surround us, cheering us on.
Their examples assure us that the finish line can be
reached. The hurdles, the trials, can be overcome
by faith. If we listen closely we can hear them say,
"If I could do it, so can you." We hear Abel call out,
telling us that the price of faithfulness is worth pay-
ing. We hear Noah's assurance that rest really does
await us at the finish line. Somewhere up ahead we
hear Abraham and Sarah, telling us to never give
up, no matter how long the road may seem. Isaac
tells us not to worry while we run the race; God
will provide everything we need. Joseph urges us
never to be satisfied with the lesser prizes offered to
us along the way. David and Samson warn us of the
pitfalls ahead, and Samuel assures us that victory is

certain. As we read their life stories we hear their voices, always cheering us onward, always encouraging us that we too can finish the race.

Our race is a marathon, not a sprint. If we are to finish we need to free ourselves of everything that holds us back or trips us up along the way. We need to get rid of unnecessary burdens that slow us down. Samson's leg of the race was cut short by the excess weight he carried with him. His example shows us that we cannot run by faith while also indulging our passions. Jacob also struggled as he ran. He never wanted to turn over the sovereignty of his life to God. Much of the pain he endured came as the Lord broke his will in an attempt to turn the schemer into a man of faith. Let's learn from his example by throwing off the weights of pride and self-willed stubbornness. We can't afford to look out for number one or hatch schemes to get what we want out of life. Life is too short and the race is too long. There is no time to waste.

We need to also watch out while we run. Nothing stops a runner faster than tripping over a hurdle or becoming entangled with another runner. During the 1984 Olympics one of America's brightest hopes for a medal in women's track, Mary Decker, lost her race when her feet became entangled with the runner she was attempting to pass. Rather than crossing the finish line in glory, her race ended as she lay on the track in pain. Hebrews 12:1 warns us to look out for the sin that "so easily entangles." I like the imagery of this verse. Sin wraps itself around our legs like vines in a jungle, and before we know it, we cannot move.

The writer of Hebrews warns us that not only

can sin entangle us, but it does so with the greatest of ease. David learned this lesson the hard way. All of his work came to a screeching halt the night he looked down from his roof and saw Bathsheba. I think he was surprised at how quickly and easily he could fall. It was as though he never realized what was happening to him. If David could fall, so can you and I. We must not be so naive as to think that we will never give in to temptation. Any one of us could be the next one to bring disgrace on the name of Christ through our actions. All of us are much more vulnerable to sin than we realize.

Therefore we need to "throw off . . . the sin that so easily entangles." The solution to sin goes beyond avoiding sources of temptation. David's trouble did not begin with the sight of Bathsheba taking a bath. The lust that moved him to commit adultery came from deep inside him. As James 1:14 warns us, "Each one is tempted when, by his own evil desire, he is dragged away and enticed." The sin that so easily entangles us begins inside of us. If we are to be free to run the race we must allow God to exchange our desires for those that flow from His heart. We must constantly allow the Holy Spirit and the Word of God to transform us in the image of Christ. Apart from a radical change on the inside, we will fall with the slightest provocation.

The race we are running can be long and difficult. The track seems to go on forever with no end in sight. Even the bravest of hearts can grow weary. What keeps us going when our legs ache and fatigue drowns out the encouragement of the spectators? Listen to the words of Hebrews 12:2–3:

Let us fix our eyes on Jesus, the author and perfecter of our faith, who for the joy set before him endured the cross, scorning its shame, and sat down at the right hand of the throne of God. Consider him who endured such opposition from sinful men, so that you will not grow weary and lose heart.

Abraham wanted to give up as his months of waiting stretched into years. Moses' parents wanted to give up as Pharaoh ordered his troops to kill all Hebrew male babies. Moses wanted to give up during his forty years of listening to the children of Israel complain. But something kept them going. They continued the race because their sights were set on a "city . . . whose architect and builder is God" (Hebrews 11:10). The prize that lay before them gave them the strength they needed to hold on to the promise by faith.

The Old Testament saints saw only a shadow of what lay ahead in comparison to all God revealed clearly in the New Testament. The prize at the finish line is more than heaven's gates. We are to fix our eyes on the One who will make heaven glorious, the One who will make all of our trials and travails seem like nothing. Our goal is to be with Jesus. The One at the right hand of the throne of God is the One who loved us so much that He gave His life for us. His example inspires us, His love amazes us, and the prospect of finally being with Him keeps us going when we would rather give up. Our goal, the prize we run for, is to be in His presence forever and ever. Now let us run. The baton has been passed.

The race is long and exhausting. In my own strength I will never finish. I pray, O Lord, for the strength and determination to run the race You have set before me. I also ask that my life will build upon the work of those who came before me. Use me to continue the eternal work You began in the lives of the heroes I admire. Take my life and glorify Your name through it. Amen.

SELECTED SCRIPTURES

Moody Press, a ministry of Moody Bible Institute,
is designed for education, evangelization, and edification.
If we may assist you in knowing more about Christ
and the Christian life, please write us without obligation:
Moody Press, c/o MLM, Chicago, Illinois 60610.